The First-Time Gardener:

CONTAINER
FOOD GARDENING

Inspiring | Educating | Creating | Entertaining

Brimming with creative inspiration, how-to projects, and useful information to enrich your everyday life, Quarto.com is a favorite destination for those pursuing their interests and passions.

First Published in 2023 by Cool Springs Press, an imprint of The Quarto Group, 100 Cummings Center, Suite 265-D, Beverly, MA 01915, USA.
T (978) 282-9590 F (978) 283-2742 Quarto.com

Cool Springs Press titles are also available at discount for retail, wholesale, promotional, and bulk purchase. For details, contact the Special Sales Manager by email at specialsales@quarto.com or by mail at The Quarto Group, Attn: Special Sales Manager, 100 Cummings Center, Suite 265-D, Beverly, MA 01915, USA.

27 26 25 24 23   1 2 3 4 5

ISBN: 978-0-7603-7813-7

Digital edition published in 2023
eISBN: 978-0-7603-7814-4

Library of Congress Cataloging-in-Publication Data is available

Design: Amy Sly and Megan Jones Design
Cover Images: Lisa Roper photographer, David Mattern, designer; courtesy of Chanticleer Garden. Christina Salwitz; Erin Farley; Mark Dwyer; George Weigel; and Stephanie Rose.
Page Layout: Megan Jones Design
Illustration: Zoe Naylor on pages 54–65 and Shutterstock on pages 1, 35, 40, 53, and 99

Printed in China

The First-Time Gardener:

CONTAINER FOOD GARDENING

ALL THE KNOW-HOW YOU NEED
TO GROW VEGGIES, FRUITS, HERBS,
AND OTHER EDIBLE PLANTS IN POTS

PAM FARLEY

COOL
SPRINGS
PRESS

To the brand new
gardeners all over the world:
You Got This! May your harvests be
spectacular and your troubles few.

Vegetables, interplanted with herbs and flowers, are a beautiful and practical addition to your container garden.

Contents

Introduction

Welcome to *The First-Time Gardener: Container Food Gardening*! This is a beginner's introduction to growing vegetables, herbs, and fruit in containers. Whether you're thinking about growing some parsley on your windowsill or setting up an extensive container garden on your apartment balcony or in your backyard, you're in the right place.

Growing food in pots or containers is the easiest way to grow a garden. You don't need a lot of space or a lot of money, and you'll get to enjoy a variety of delicious, fresh foods. You might even find your kids eating snap peas right off the vine, like mine do!

My name is Pam Farley, and I've been container gardening in my city backyard for more than 25 years. Some years, we grow more food than we can eat—and some years, things don't turn out so well. But each year I keep trying, and I'm always learning new things. I share my successes and failures in the garden on my website, BrownThumbMama.com.

After all these years in the garden, I've learned a lot about what works—and even more about what doesn't work. Some of the gardening advice you'll hear out there is inaccurate at best and harmful at worst. This book will bust some of those myths and help you get your container garden started right. You'll benefit from my years of experience, and you'll grow your gardening confidence along with your vegetables.

Vegetables can be pruned and trained to grow in the smallest spaces, like this balcony garden with a potted cucumber growing on a trellis.

Welcome to the world of gardening! I'm so glad you're here.

The First-Time Gardener: Container Food Gardening starts at the very beginning and answers the questions that other gardening books assume you know. Things like

- What does "full sun" mean?

- Is there a "right side up" when you plant seeds?

- Should I start my garden with seeds or plants from the nursery?

- Do I really need all those fancy tools and gizmos to start a garden?

I promise you'll find the answers to these questions and many, many more throughout these pages. You can read this book straight through from beginning to end or use the table of contents or index to skip from one section to another as needed throughout the growing season.

Once you've started your garden, I'd love to see what you've grown! Share with me (@BrownThumbMama) on Facebook or Instagram and use the tag #ContainerFoodGardening.

Happy gardening!

You can grow container vegetables in the front yard, and no one will be any the wiser. This potted artichoke plant is surrounded by colorful violas with parsley growing below.

1

Why Grow Your Own Food?

When I got my own place after college, I told my friends I was starting a vegetable garden. Some of them scoffed. "You have a nice office job and are planning your wedding. You have too much going on! Why would you spend all that time and trouble planting a garden when you can just buy what you want at the store?"

As you may suspect, I planted that garden anyway. Even though I had a busy schedule, it only took a few minutes each day to tend to the garden. It was a little nature break in my own backyard, and I would munch on snow peas and strawberries while petting the neighbor's cat. Gardening is relaxing and productive, all at the same time. There's nothing better than enjoying your harvest—whether your plant produces only a single tomato or you end up with more green beans than your family can eat in a month.

Regardless of whether you decide to grow a few herbs on your windowsill or to plant every single one of your favorite vegetables, you'll soon find that growing your own food is one of the most amazing and satisfying pastimes out there. Here are some reasons why:

FRESH IS BEST

Did you know that some of the vegetables at the grocery store are picked weeks before you buy them? Many fruits and vegetables are grown in other countries and shipped to warehouses before being trucked to the store. Some fruits, like apples, are held in cold storage for months until they're sent to the produce department. This means you aren't enjoying them at their best flavor or freshness. Compare that to being able to walk out to your patio, pick an apple off your tree, and eat it on the spot. Yes, you can grow fruit trees in containers! Check out Chapter 2 for details.

AMAZING VARIETY

How many types of carrots can you find at your grocery store or farmer's market—maybe two or three? Believe it or not, there are more than 40 different varieties of carrots that you can grow and enjoy. And there are thousands of types of tomatoes, in nearly every color and size you can imagine. There are even striped and spotted tomatoes! Growing a garden is the best way to try unique and delicious vegetables. You might find yourself at the store, looking at the price of an unusual herb or vegetable, and deciding to grow it for yourself for much less.

FAMILY FUN

Kids who grow vegetables and fruits love to eat them. There's nothing better than sharing a few hours in the garden with the kids in your life—even the youngest toddlers can drop a seed into a pot and sprinkle it with water. The kids will enjoy a reason to play in the dirt, and along with their vegetables they'll grow a lifelong love of gardening. You'll save a ton of money (especially if your kids eat as much fruit as mine do). And they'll be the talk of the lunchroom when they show up with homegrown purple snow peas, white alpine strawberries, or yellow carrots.

SAFETY & HEALTH

Every so often, you'll hear a news story about a vegetable recall due to contamination of some sort. People and stores end up throwing away huge amounts of spinach, sprouts, lettuce, or other vegetables because of safety concerns. If you're growing your own vegetables and fruits, the chances of contamination are nearly zero. You can decide if you want to grow using organic principles, conventional fertilizers, or a combination of both.

ENVIRONMENTAL IMPACT

Almost everything in the grocery store comes from farms and warehouses that are hundreds or even thousands of miles away. When you grow your own herbs, vegetables, and fruits, you're helping in a small way to reduce shipping pollution. No plastic packaging is required for homegrown food, which also reduces waste—plus, when you share your harvest with your friends and neighbors, you're building community and saving them from a trip to the store. Your outdoor container garden also provides a habitat for birds, bees, butterflies, and other bugs. If you choose to plant in recycled or upcycled containers, you're keeping those items out of the waste stream, as well.

What the heck does that word mean?

Don't fret! All of us were new gardeners at some point, and no question is silly or dumb. If you run across a gardening word you don't recognize, check the Glossary on page 166 for a clear and simple definition. And if you have a question that this book doesn't answer, send it to me at BrownThumbMama.com/contact and I'll answer the most popular questions in future articles!

Golden sage has striking, variegated leaves that are edible and ornamental.

Container gardening allows you to grow a wide variety of unique and delicious vegetables, like these beautiful heirloom tomatoes.

With a little care, your container garden will be quite prolific. These four melon plants yielded more than 20 melons!

Advantages of Container Gardening

Seriously, container gardening is like magic. Living in a tiny duplex? Floating along the river on a houseboat? Sitting by the window of your 32nd-floor apartment? No problem. You can have a garden! All you need is a pot, seeds, and soil. Growing food in containers is fantastic for people without a lot of space, and it's great for regular gardeners too. Here are some of the reasons why you'll fall in love with container gardening:

BEAUTIFUL

Container gardens are beautiful, no matter your aesthetic. You might choose sleek and modern containers, use wood and metal for a rustic look, or go vintage with upcycled antiques. Some gardeners use a stunning container plant as a focal point for their traditional garden. The most amazing part of container gardens, however, is that there are virtually no weeds. Traditional gardeners can spend hours weeding—but you'll spend **your** hours enjoying your beautiful, easy-to-maintain garden.

PORTABLE

Having portable plants comes in handy, sometimes when you least expect it. If your landlord cancels your lease—pack up the garden, move, and keep on growing. Is a freeze or a hailstorm coming your way? Bring your plants inside to protect them from the weather. If you notice that a particular plant has a bug problem, you can isolate that container before you have a *major garden infestation* (ask me how I know). And best of all, containers make it easy to grow food everywhere. If the neighbors or the HOA get upset about your front yard chard, just move the planter to the backyard!

ACCESSIBLE

My parents were physically disabled, and they were container gardeners out of necessity. They couldn't plant or till in the ground, so they planted vegetables in pots on

This compact sweet pea bush will thrive on a tiny apartment patio or in an expansive backyard.

Container gardens, like this salad blend, can be moved inside during a freeze or placed on a table for easier access.

a backyard table. Container growing is a great solution for gardeners with physical limitations. Set planters on a bench to reduce bending and stooping, or place them on a table that a wheelchair user can roll right up to. Larger containers can sit on the soil, keeping walking paths clear for walkers, canes, and wheelchairs. Stackable container gardens have a small footprint, which is perfect for a senior's apartment or assisted living facility. These tall gardens allow you to grow many different plants on a small patio.

Living walls are a great option too. They require no bending to plant or harvest.

Do vegetable plants regrow every year?

Good question! You might wonder if you need to buy new vegetable plants or seeds each year, and the answer is (mostly) yes.

Most vegetables and herbs are **annuals**, which means they complete their life cycle in one growing season. They grow, produce food, flower, set seed, and die within a year of planting. Examples of annual vegetables include beans, cucumber, lettuce, radish, and watermelon.

Many fruit-producing trees, bushes, and smaller plants are **perennials**, which means they will grow and produce for years with proper care. Blueberries, apples, and strawberries are all perennials. There are a handful of perennial vegetables too; rhubarb and asparagus are two good examples.

Note: Some garden vegetables, like tomatoes, peppers, and eggplants, are perennials—but since they can't survive a frost, most gardeners grow them as annuals.

There are a few herbs and vegetables that are **biennial**. Plants in this category grow leaves their first year and flowers their second year. We usually eat them before they go to flower, though. Kale, beets, and parsley are biennial plants.

Peppers, like this purple variety, are grown as an annual in vegetable gardens because they do not survive frosts, but in tropical climates without freezing temperatures, they are a perennial.

Planting from Seedlings vs. Planting from Seed

How do you know whether you should plant seeds, seedlings, or larger (more mature) plants? Some vegetables grow best when planted from seed, and some can be bought only as seedlings or mature plants. The chart on pages 32–35 will show you which is best for the plants you want to grow.

Here are some things to remember when you head to the garden store.

SEEDLINGS

Seedlings (also called starts or transplants) are sold in 4- or 6-pack containers or smaller pots. These plants have been started from seed in a greenhouse or nursery. They give you a couple-week head start on sowing seed in your garden and are easy to transplant, which is a big advantage for a new gardener. There are some vegetables and herbs that are hard to grow from seed, so seedlings are the way to go.

The downside of planting transplants is that there might not be much variety in the seedlings you can get at your local nursery. There might be only one or two varieties of tomato, and one type of squash. Seedlings are also more expensive than seeds since much of the work has been done by the nursery staff.

What to Look for When Buying Seedlings

Most of the time, the seedlings you get at the nursery are going to be strong and healthy. But it's always a good idea to choose your seedlings carefully and know what to look for and what to avoid.

Your seedlings should be healthy and green. No yellowing leaves allowed! It's also best to choose a short, leafy seedling instead of one with a long, skinny stem and only a couple of leaves. Check under the leaves for bugs—you don't want to accidentally bring home a pest.

Seedlings from the garden center are an easy way to get a head start on your garden. Look for short, leafy plants like this strawberry instead of tall stems with few leaves.

LARGER PLANTS

Larger plants often seem like a great deal—they may already have flowers or fruits growing on them. Don't buy *annual* vegetables as a larger plant, though. Since they've been in a smaller-than-optimal container for most of their life cycle, they may not thrive in your garden. If they're your only option, remove all the flowers and immature vegetables after planting it in the appropriately sized container. This way, the plant can focus its energy on growing strong roots in the short term so it will make more food in the long term.

When buying *perennial* fruits or vegetables, larger plants are the best choice. They're more mature and will therefore produce more quickly after they're planted into a larger container in the garden.

What to Look for When Buying Larger Plants

Professional growers have raised the larger plants at the nursery, so they'll be healthy and ready to transplant when you take them home. There are a few things to look out for, though.

Find out when the delivery days are and try to shop on those days. That way, you'll get the newest, freshest, strongest plants. These mature plants should be robust, with dark green leaves. Don't buy a larger plant that's wilted or has brown leaves. Check under the leaves for bugs, and gently tip the plant out of the container (if you can) to ensure the plant isn't root bound.

Larger, nursery-grown plants that already have fruit on them are not the best bet since they are likely to suffer from more transplant shock when you move them into their new home.

SEEDS

Seeds are much cheaper than seedlings—for just a few dollars, you can get a packet of seeds that will grow many, many plants. There's a lot of planting information on the seed packet, and you can get additional information on my website (BrownThumbMama.com) or the seed company's website.

There are infinitely more varieties to choose from in a seed catalog than at a nursery—which can be fun or overwhelming, depending on your personality. Seeds will keep for a few years if stored in a cool, dark place, and you can share seeds with neighbors, friends, and other gardeners. This is called a "seed swap," and is a fun way to meet other gardeners and grow new varieties of plants.

What to Look for When Buying Seeds

If you're buying from a reputable seed company or local nursery, you'll get healthy seeds that were stored carefully and will grow well.

If you see a great deal on seeds at the grocery store or mega-mart, you should check a few things before buying. Flip the packet over and check for the information in the next section.

How to Read a Seed Packet

Seed packets are a miniguide to your plants' needs. While packets can't explain everything in detail like a book or website can, there's still lots of helpful information on those little envelopes. I keep my seeds grouped by type (vegetable, herb, flower), which makes it easy to flip through my seed box and figure out what to plant next.

SEED PACKET INFORMATION

Some seed companies pack a lot of information on their seed packets, and some just list the plant's name. Here are the must-have pieces of information your seed packet should tell you:

Plant name and picture: There are many different varieties of zucchini, for example, and you might want to plant them all—so you'll need to keep track of the varieties you plant. A photo or drawing of the mature plant will help you recognize it immediately in your seed box.

Container-specific types: There isn't an industry standard for container plant names. You might find a note on the seed packet that says, "great for containers," but don't panic if that's not explicitly listed. When looking for container plants, watch for any of these words in the name: compact, bush, tiny, baby, midget, dwarf, or teeny.

Days to maturity: This is important because stores will keep selling seeds long after it's too late to plant them. For example, if your area gets cold in early September and you're buying watermelon seeds in July, they won't have enough time to grow and ripen before frost hits.

Seed count: Seed packaging isn't always consistent—some packets list the weight of the seeds, and some give a seed count. If the plant is rare or difficult to grow, you may only get 8 or 10 seeds in a packet. Most common vegetable seeds like squash, peas, and carrots have 30 to 40 seeds in a packet.

Seeds are the most economical way to start your garden. You can grow a lot of unique varieties of vegetables with just a few seed packets.

Planting instructions: Instructions on the packet are brief, and they'll give you a head start on planting. They should include how deep to plant the seed, when to plant, how far apart to plant, and how quickly the seeds will germinate.

Date: All vegetable seed packets should list the year they were packed, and/or have a "Packed for (year)" date stamped on them. If the "Packed for" date is last year or before, don't buy the seeds. While some seeds will remain viable for a couple of years, it's best to buy new seeds that are packed for the current year.

Seed type: Finally, the seed packet should indicate if the seeds are organic or conventional (if it doesn't say, they're conventional). If the seeds are heirloom, open-pollinated, or hybrid that will be listed too.

Types of Seeds

When I was little, my grandma and I would walk to the five-and-dime so she could pick out 10-cent seed packets from a spinner rack. Nowadays, gardeners are much more likely to order seeds online or from a seed catalog (a favorite for winter reading when the days are dark and cold).

There are a few different types of seeds, and you may find different reasons to choose different types. Over time, you'll figure out which seed companies and types you like the best, and which seed brands grow best in your garden.

Organic: Organic seeds are grown according to mandated organic standards. This includes inspecting the fields and ensuring that no synthetic fertilizers, pesticides, fungicides, or other prohibited chemicals are used on the plants. If you buy organic seeds, you can use conventional garden products on them without harming the plants (if you follow label directions). Organic seeds are often more costly than nonorganic seeds, so gardeners who make this added investment are, more often than not, interested in growing their plants organically from seed to harvest.

Hybrids: Hybrid seeds or plants are made by crossing two closely related plants (this is completely different from GMO seeds). This cross-pollination has always happened in nature, and plant breeders have been intentionally crossbreeding plants for decades. Plants are bred for certain characteristics like uniform size, earlier maturity, disease resistance, and so on. Seedless watermelons are one example of a hybrid. The catch with hybrid plants is that if you save the seeds to plant next year, because of the cross-pollination, they won't grow "true to type."

Open pollinated: Open pollination occurs when plants are freely pollinated by birds, bugs, wind, or other natural methods. The advantage of using open-pollinated seeds is that you can save seeds from this year's plants to grow next year. After years of seed saving and replanting, open-pollinated plants will become better adapted to their local growing conditions and climate.

Heirloom: Just like an heirloom clock passed down through the family, heirloom seeds are passed down from one generation to another over time. They're often tied to a specific geographical location or ethnic group. Heirloom plants are all open pollinated, but not all open-pollinated plants are heirlooms. These fruits and vegetables aren't

Planting from seed is quick and simple. Some seeds should be started indoors while others can be directly seeded into their outdoor container.

usually found in the supermarket because they don't meet market requirements. They might be too fragile to ship or have a short shelf life.

GMO (Genetically Modified Organism): GMO plants are created by introducing genes from unrelated species in a laboratory. This usually involves adding or deleting genes to create specific traits, like pest resistance, longer shelf life, or increased nutritional value. At the time of this writing, home gardeners can't buy GMO seeds because they're created for the industrial agriculture market and their sale is regulated.

Proper seed storage can enhance the life of your seeds.

How to Store Seeds

As you know, seeds will grow when they're in a warm, moist environment (your garden). Therefore, the best way to store them is to keep them cool and dry, so they remain dormant. I keep my seeds in a wooden box in the pantry. You could also store your seeds in the refrigerator, cupboard, or closet.

There are lots of containers you can use for seed storage. Some people store seed packets in large canning jars, and some use plastic shoebox-sized containers. I've seen gardeners with extensive seed collections using plastic, compartmentalized photo storage containers. All the squash seed packets are in one container, the peas are in another, and so on. These small containers then fit into a larger storage box.

Please don't keep your seeds outside or in the garage. Critters like mice could eat your seeds, and snails and slugs will eat the paper packets. The temperature and humidity changes can also damage the seeds and prevent them from growing.

Seed life

You don't have to plant every single seed you have this year—most seeds will last for a few years when stored properly. If you find a packet of seeds in your collection that's out of date, don't throw it away. Toss the seeds in a corner of the garden or make a "mystery pot" and see what sprouts. You may be pleasantly surprised!

REPLACE EACH YEAR	REPLACE AFTER 2 YEARS	REPLACE AFTER 4 YEARS	REPLACE AFTER 5 YEARS
Chives	Arugula	Beets	Artichokes
Corn	Asparagus	Chard	Celery
Garlic	Beans	Eggplant	Collards
Leek	Broccoli	Fennel	Cucumbers
Onion	Brussels sprouts	Kale	Lettuce
Parsley	Cabbage	Kohlrabi	Melons
Parsnip	Carrots	Mustard	Radish
Shallot	Cauliflower	Pumpkins	Turnips
	Celery	Rutabagas	
	Okra	Summer squash	
	Peas	Tomatoes	
	Peppers	Watermelon	
	Spinach	Winter squash	

How to Plant a Seedling or Larger Plant

1   Gather your materials: the pot of your choice, container soil, and the seedling(s). When planting a larger plant, you may also want a hand shovel.

2   Fill the pot to about 1 inch (2.5 cm) from the top with moist potting soil. Decide where the seedling will go (center of the pot, off to one side, etc.) and scoop some soil out. Because your soil is moist, the sides of the hole should not crumble in.

3   Nestle the seedling, nursery container and all, into this hole. This will confirm that you've removed enough soil for the plant and its roots to fit comfortably. If the nursery container fits only partly into the hole, remove more soil. If the top of the nursery container is lower than the surrounding soil, add more soil to the hole.

4   Remove the seedling and container from the hole. Now it's time to remove the seedling from the container. Please don't pull the plant by the stem! Seedlings are tender little babies, and this can cause the stem to break or rip the roots. Put your hand over the top of the container, on either side of the plant's stem. Tip the container sideways and gently squeeze it. The plant and soil will loosen and slip out into your hand.

5 Once the plant is out of the container, it's important to loosen the roots so they can spread out into the pot you're using. Use your fingers to gently untangle the soil and the roots—especially if the roots are circling around and around. It's okay if some of the tiny roots break but try not to damage the larger ones.

6 Place the seedling in the hole and check its position. Is it sitting lower than the rest of the soil? Gently lift the seedling out and put more soil under it. Is it higher than the rest of the soil? Either remove soil from under it or spread the roots out more.

7 Press lightly on the soil right around the stem. Add a bit of soil if needed to even out the soil level. Pour water gently around the plant using a watering can or cup. A strong blast of water from the hose can blow the seedling right out of the pot.

8 Congratulations! You've transplanted your seedling and it's ready to grow and thrive.

How to Plant a Seed

1 Gather your materials: the container of your choice filled with moistened potting soil and the seeds.

2 Check the seed packet to determine how deep to plant the seeds, and how far apart each seed should be placed. Using your finger, a pencil, or a small stick, make a hole in the soil for the seed.

3 Stop! Take a look at the seeds in the packet. Most of the time they'll be whole and healthy, like the seeds on the top of this photo. Don't plant seeds that are discolored, broken in half, or feel flat and empty, like the seeds on the bottom. Give yourself the best chance for success by planting the healthiest seeds.

4 Drop the seed into the hole. It doesn't matter which direction the seed is facing—seeds don't have a "right side up."

5 Plant all the seeds in the container before covering them over with soil.

6 Smooth the soil over the hole, covering the seed completely. Pat the soil over the seed gently to make sure the seed won't wash away.

7 Gently and slowly water the container with a watering can or rain wand. A strong blast of water from the hose can wash the seeds right out of the pot. Keep the soil moist until the seeds sprout; if the top layer of soil hardens into a crust, the seeds might not be able to grow through it.

8 In just a short time, your seeds will sprout and fill up your container.

Essential container gardening tools

It's entirely possible to be lured in by all the fancy garden tools at your local nursery, but you only need a few tools for container gardening. These are my must-have container gardening tools:

1. **Gardening gloves:** Sturdy gloves are a must. They keep your hands clean and dry, prevent blisters and cuts, and keep bacteria from getting into small cuts or abrasions. If you don't like traditional gardening gloves, wear thin medical gloves.

2. **CobraHead® weeder/cultivator:** This is an amazing tool for loosening soil, planting, and weeding. It's like a curved fingernail that gets into tight spaces—which is perfect for container gardening.

3. **Heavy-duty trowel (hand shovel):** Inexpensive aluminum trowels can break easily, so I use a stainless-steel trowel that won't bend or break.

4. **Watering device (hose, watering can, sprinkler system):** I have a heavy-duty metal watering can because it's durable and has a handle on the top and the side, making it easy to pour.

RIGHT: There are a few essential tools for container gardening. A good trowel and a hose or watering can are two of them.

Ladybugs are a welcome visitor to the garden.
This one's inspecting a young basil seedling
in a vertical planter.

2

Decide What to Grow

When you open your first seed catalog, or visit the garden center in the spring, the choices can be overwhelming. There are literally thousands of plants you can choose from—how do you know what to pick? Gardening should be fun and not stressful. Here are some tips to help you get your container garden started.

GROW WHAT YOU LIKE TO EAT

While this seems obvious, it's advice that gardeners don't always follow. My dad was famous for growing chard, even though he never wanted to eat it. When I asked him why, he said, "Well, it's one of the few things I can get to grow. But once I tried it, I'll be darned if I didn't like it." Think about which vegetables your family likes and grow those.

Do you buy herbs each week at the grocery store? They're often $2 a bunch or more. Instead, you could grow a few herbs on your windowsill, have a nearly endless supply, and save lots of money. If you like specialty vegetables that aren't readily available in your area, like daikon, jicama, cucamelon, and so on—grow those in your container garden.

PLANT FOR OPTIMAL RETURN

This reminds me of the phrase "return on investment" from my corporate days. In the garden, it means that you should choose the best plants for the space you have available. For example: artichokes are beautiful and easy to grow, but they need a large container and produce only a few chokes per plant. If you only have space for one big container, it's better to plant an assortment of vegetables instead of one single artichoke.

THINK LONG TERM

Since your container garden is portable, consider planting fruit trees or perennials that will come back year after year. If you move to a new place, bring them along. It can take a year or two for fruit trees or perennials to produce, but with a little care you'll be harvesting for years. And there's nothing in the world like eating a crisp, juicy apple picked right off your tree.

GROW ORGANIC

If eating organic food is important to you, container gardening allows you to ensure that every part of the process is organic. You can buy organic seeds, soil, and fertilizer, and use natural pest control methods. The Environmental Working Group (www.ewg.org) shares which conventionally grown fruits and vegetables are most likely to contain pesticide residue at ewg.org/foodnews/dirty-dozen.php. If your family likes any of these fruits or vegetables high on the list, you can easily grow them organically in your container garden.

These columnar apple trees in pots are ideal for small spaces and containers.

Identifying Container Gardening Plants

While you can grow some full-sized plants in containers, they'll probably have reduced yield due to the confined space of the container. You'll get the strongest plants and the best harvest if you choose plants specifically bred for container gardening. Search your favorite seed company's website for "container garden," or look for plants with the words *compact*, *bush*, *tiny*, *baby*, *midget*, *dwarf*, or *teeny* in their name.

Watermelon selections, like 'Sugar Baby', have compact vines and do well in pots.

RIGHT: When choosing plants for your container garden, look for words like "tiny" or "compact" in the name. This cucumber produces standard-size fruit on a compact vine.

Quick Planting Guide

This chart will give you a quick guide to the easiest container plants for beginners. You can see immediately what container size you'll need; whether the plant is best planted from seed or starts; and its sun, water, and fertilizer needs.

If you like to be superorganized, set a reminder on your phone (or make a note on your calendar) so you know when it's time to plant and fertilize. Then you won't expend precious brain cells trying to remember the schedule. You can also put a potential harvest date on the calendar, so you know when to start planning meals around your harvest!

Note: Vegetables that are more challenging to grow, like carrots, broccoli, jicama, and others, aren't listed here. You can learn about how to grow them on my website, BrownThumbMama.com.

Herbs, vegetables, and flowers are a lovely and colorful combination for your container garden.

PLANT	CONTAINER SIZE PER 1 PLANT	WHEN TO PLANT	SEED OR START	SUN	WATER	FERTILIZER	HARVEST
Bush Bean	3 gallon (14 L) or larger	After last spring frost—succession plant every 2 weeks.	Seed	Full sun	Water well until established and then provide regular water. Don't get water on leaves.	Half-strength fertilizer every 2 weeks.	55–60 days. Harvest when beans are firm and about the diameter of a pencil.
Beet	1 gallon (5 L) or larger; at least 10" (25 cm) deep	3–4 weeks before last spring frost and/or in the fall—succession plant every 2–3 weeks.	Seed	Full sun to partial shade	Water well until established and then provide regular water.	Each week during the growing season.	45–65 days. Harvest leaves anytime; pull beets when about 1.5" (4 cm) in diameter.
Chard	1 gallon (5 L) or larger	2–3 weeks before last spring frost.	Either	Full sun to partial shade	Water well until established and then provide regular water.	Once or twice during the growing season.	20–60 days. Cut outer leaves when 6–8" (15–20 cm) tall and allow inner leaves to grow.

PLANT	CONTAINER SIZE PER 1 PLANT	WHEN TO PLANT	SEED OR START	SUN	WATER	FERTILIZER	HARVEST
Cucamelon	5 gallon (23 L) or larger. Will need a trellis or other support.	2 weeks after last spring frost.	Start	Full sun	Water well until established and then provide regular water.	Once a month during the growing season.	70–75 days. Harvest when 1 inch (2.5 cm) in size, before seeds develop.
Cucumber	5 gallon (23 L) or larger, at least 10" (25 cm) deep. Will need a trellis or other support.	1–2 weeks after last spring frost.	Either	Full sun	Water well until established and then provide regular water. Don't let the soil dry out or they'll be bitter and hollow.	Each week during the growing season.	60–70 days. Cut off the vine when cucumber is small.
Eggplant	5 gallon (23 L) or larger, at least 10" (25 cm) deep	2 weeks after last spring frost.	Start	Full sun	Water well until established and then provide regular water.	Half-strength fertilizer every 2 weeks.	75–90 days. Harvest when fruit is small and feels heavy for size. Cut with scissors or pruners.
Garlic	3 gallon (14 L) or larger, at least 6" (15 cm) deep	In fall	Garlic cloves	Full sun	Water well while sprouting and new leaves are forming. Reduce water when leaves begin to die back.	Every other week during the growing season.	8 months. Harvest when nearly all leaves have turned brown. Don't pull the plant but dig up with a shovel.
Green onion	1 gallon (5 L) or larger	2 weeks before last spring frost	Either	Full sun to partial shade	Water well until established and then provide regular water.	Every other week during the growing season.	60 days. Cut off green part with scissors or pull entire plant when the thickness of a pencil.
Kale	3 gallon (14 L) or larger	3–4 weeks before last spring frost (fall/winter in hot summer areas).	Either	Full sun to partial shade	Water well until established and then provide regular water.	Once or twice during the growing season.	45–60 days. Harvest individual leaves from outside of plant when about the size of your hand.

PLANT	CONTAINER SIZE PER 1 PLANT	WHEN TO PLANT	SEED OR START	SUN	WATER	FERTILIZER	HARVEST
Lettuce	3 gallon (14 L) or larger	4 weeks before last spring frost, succession plant every 2 weeks.	Either	Full sun to partial shade	Water well until established and then provide regular water. Lettuce has shallow roots, so don't let the soil dry out.	Once or twice during the growing season.	21–50 days. Harvest individual leaves or cut entire plant just above the soil line.
Okra	5 gallon (23 L) or larger and at least 10" (25 cm) deep	2 weeks after last spring frost.	Seed	Full sun	Water well until established and then provide regular water.	No	50–65 days. Harvest pods at 2–3" (5–8 cm) long. Cut with scissors or pruners.
Pea	1 gallon (5 L) or larger. Will need a trellis or other support.	5 weeks before last spring frost.	Seed	Full sun to partial shade	Water well until established and then provide regular water.	Once or twice during the growing season.	60–70 days. Harvest when young and pick often to encourage production.
Pepper (sweet or hot)	5 gallon (23 L) or larger	2 weeks after last spring frost.	Start	Full sun	Water well until established and then provide regular, consistent water. Don't get water on leaves.	Phosphorus-rich fertilizer every 2 weeks.	Sweet peppers: 70–90 days; hot peppers: 70–100 days. Cut peppers from plant with pruners or scissors. Frequent harvesting encourages production.
Potato	At least 5 gallon (23 L) and 18" (46 cm) wide, 2' (60 cm) deep	2 weeks after last spring frost, or late fall in warm summer locations.	Seed potatoes	Full sun	Water well until established and then provide regular water. Soil should not be overly wet or potatoes will rot.	Once or twice during the growing season.	90–120 days. After plant develops flowers and foliage dies back, carefully dump out the container to harvest.

PLANT	CONTAINER SIZE PER 1 PLANT	WHEN TO PLANT	SEED OR START	SUN	WATER	FERTILIZER	HARVEST
Radish	½ gallon (3 L) or larger	3 weeks before last spring frost, succession plant every week.	Seed	Full sun to partial shade	Water well until established and then provide regular water.	Not usually necessary.	25–60 days. Harvest when small by pulling gently out of the soil.
Summer squash	5 gallon (23 L) or larger	After last spring frost.	Seed	Full sun	Water well until established and then provide regular, consistent water. Don't get water on leaves.	Phosphorus-rich fertilizer monthly.	45–60 days. Harvest when squash are small; cut stem with pruner or sharp knife.
Tomato	10 gallon (45 L) or larger. Will need a tomato cage or other support.	After last spring frost.	Start	Full sun	Water thoroughly and consistently. Don't let soil dry out, and don't get water on leaves.	Liquid seaweed fertilizer every 1–2 weeks during the growing season.	60–100 days. Cut or gently pull tomatoes from plant when deep red and firm.

Blueberries are ideal for container gardening since they need special fertilizer for acid-loving plants.

Fruit Planting Guide

PLANT	CONTAINER SIZE	WHEN TO PLANT	SEED OR START	SUN	WATER	FERTILIZER	HARVEST
Apple	20 gallon (91 L) or larger; may need to repot as the tree grows.	In spring after frost danger has passed.	Tree from nursery	Full sun	Check the soil weekly; if dry, apply water slowly to allow it to soak in.	Apply at planting, then usually not needed until tree is bearing fruit. At that point, apply during growing season.	Up to 1–3 years after planting. Taste to ensure ripeness and pull gently when apples reach their full, bright color.
Apricot	15 gallon (68 L) or larger; may need to repot as the tree grows.	In spring after frost danger has passed.	Tree from nursery	Full sun	Water weekly until established. Then check the soil weekly; if dry, apply water slowly to allow it to soak in.	Apply liquid fertilizer in spring and summer.	Up to 1–2 years after planting. Ripe fruit will release with a gentle twist.
Avocado	15 gallon (68 L) or larger; may need to repot as the tree grows.	In spring after frost danger has passed.	Tree from nursery	Full sun; in cold climates, bring indoors during winter.	Check the soil weekly; if dry, apply water slowly to allow it to soak in.	Apply at planting, then usually not needed until tree is bearing fruit. At that point, apply during growing season.	Up to 2–3 years after planting. Pick when fruit has rusty-brown specks or skin dulls, then bring inside to ripen.
Blackberry	10 gallon (45 L) or larger.	In spring after frost danger has passed.	Bush from nursery	Full sun	Water well until established and then provide regular, consistent water.	In spring and just after harvest.	Up to 1 year after planting. Gently pull from plant when berries are fully dark.
Blueberry	10 gallon (45 L) or larger; at least 18" (46 cm) wide and deep.	In spring after frost danger has passed.	Bush from nursery. Needs potting soil for acid-loving plants (e.g., azalea, rhododendron).	Full sun with afternoon shade in warm climates.	Consistent moisture without standing water.	Monthly with fertilizer for acid-loving plants.	Up to 1 year after planting. Pick when berries turn deep blue and fall into your hand when lightly brushed.

PLANT	CONTAINER SIZE	WHEN TO PLANT	SEED OR START	SUN	WATER	FERTILIZER	HARVEST
Cantaloupe	5 gallon (23 L) or larger and at least 18" (46 cm) wide and deep. Will need a trellis or other support.	1–2 weeks after last spring frost.	Either	Full sun	Water well until established and then provide regular, consistent water. Don't get water on leaves.	Once a month during the growing season.	80–90 days. When ripe, will easily slip from vine with a gentle pull.
Cherry	20 gallon (91 L) or larger; may need to repot as the tree grows.	In spring after frost danger has passed.	Tree from nursery	Full sun	Check the soil weekly; if dry, apply water slowly to allow it to soak in.	Apply a low-nitrogen fertilizer in early spring.	Up to 3–4 years after planting. Harvest when firm and fully red; cut with pruner, leaving stems attached to fruit.
Citrus	20 gallon (91 L) or larger; may need to repot as the tree grows.	In spring after frost danger has passed.	Trees from nursery	Full sun; may need shade during the hottest part of the day in warm climates.	Water well until established and then provide regular water. Allow top 2" (5 cm) of soil to dry out before watering again.	Apply citrus fertilizer each month during the growing season.	Up to 1 year after planting. Cut stem with pruner, don't pull fruit off the tree.
Fig	15 gallon (68 L) or larger.	In spring after frost danger has passed.	Tree from nursery	Full sun; in cold climates, bring indoors during winter.	Check the soil weekly; if dry, apply water slowly to allow it to soak in.	Apply at planting, then usually not needed until tree is bearing fruit. At that point, apply diluted fish emulsion weekly.	Up to 1 year after planting. Harvest frequently, when fruits are brownish purple. Cut stem with pruner.
Grape	15 gallon (68 L) or larger; will need a trellis or other support.	In spring after frost danger has passed.	1-year-old vine from nursery	At least 6 hours of sun	Water well until established and then provide regular, consistent water.	Fertilize with compost in spring.	Up to 1 year after planting. Taste to ensure ripeness and cut from vine with pruner.

PLANT	CONTAINER SIZE	WHEN TO PLANT	SEED OR START	SUN	WATER	FERTILIZER	HARVEST
Nectarine	20 gallon (91 L) or larger; may need to repot as the tree grows.	In spring after frost danger has passed.	Tree from nursery	Full sun	Check the soil weekly; if dry, apply water slowly to allow it to soak in.	Apply at planting, then usually not needed until tree is bearing fruit. At that point, apply during growing season.	From 2–4 years after planting. Harvest when there are no more traces of green and the fruit is slightly soft. Twist while pulling away from the branch.
Peach	20 gallon (91 L) or larger; may need to repot as the tree grows.	In spring after frost danger has passed.	Tree from nursery	Full sun	Check the soil weekly; if dry, apply water slowly to allow it to soak in.	Apply at planting, then usually not needed until tree is bearing fruit. At that point, apply during growing season.	From 2–4 years after planting. Harvest when there are no more traces of green and the fruit is slightly soft. Twist while pulling away from the branch.
Pear	20 gallon (91 L) or larger; may need to repot as the tree grows.	In spring after frost danger has passed.	Tree from nursery	6–8 hours of sun	Check the soil weekly; if dry, apply water slowly to allow it to soak in.	Apply at planting, then usually not needed until tree is bearing fruit. At that point, apply during growing season.	Up to 4–6 years after planting. Harvest when hard and yellow-green, then bring inside to ripen.
Plum	20 gallon (91 L) or larger; may need to repot as the tree grows.	In spring after frost danger has passed.	Tree from nursery	Full sun	Check the soil weekly; if dry, apply water slowly to allow it to soak in.	Apply at planting, then usually not needed until tree is bearing fruit. At that point, apply during growing season.	From 3–6 years after planting. Harvest when a gentle twist separates the fruit from the branch.
Raspberry	10 gallon (45 L) or larger	In spring after frost danger has passed.	Bush from nursery	Full sun	Water well until established and then provide regular, consistent water.	Once a month during the growing season.	Up to 1 year after planting. Gently pull from plant when berries are fully red.

PLANT	CONTAINER SIZE	WHEN TO PLANT	SEED OR START	SUN	WATER	FERTILIZER	HARVEST
Strawberry	3 gallon (14 L) or larger; or use container with cutouts on the side	4 weeks before last spring frost.	Start	Full sun; partial shade in very hot climates.	Water well until established and then provide regular, consistent water. Use mulch to retain soil moisture.	Every 2 weeks during the growing season.	Up to 1 year after planting. Cut or gently pull from plant when berries are firm and fully red.
Watermelon	10 gallon (45 L) or larger and at least 18" wide and deep.	In spring after frost danger has passed.	Either	Full sun	Water well until established and then provide regular, thorough water. Don't let the soil become completely dry and don't get water on leaves.	Once a month during the growing season.	80–90 days. Cut from vine when curlicue tendril next to melon is dry and brown.

Grow herbs in separate pots or combine them into one container to make a countertop herb garden.

Herb Planting Guide

PLANT	CONTAINER SIZE	WHEN TO PLANT	SEED OR START	SUN	WATER	FERTILIZER	HARVEST
Basil	2 gallon (9 L) or larger	In spring after frost danger has passed.	Either	Full sun	Thoroughly until established and then allow to dry a little between watering.	Once or twice during the growing season.	30 days from start; 60–90 days from seed. Pick off leaves once the plant is 4–6" (10–15 cm) tall
Bay	15 gallon (68 L) or larger; may need to repot as it grows.	In spring after frost danger has passed.	Tree or bush from nursery	Full sun; in cold climates, bring indoors during winter.	Keep soil barely moist until established and then water occasionally.	Fertilize in spring.	Harvest leaves any time (evergreen), mature leaves are dark green and leathery
Chive	2 gallon (9 L) or larger	In spring after frost danger has passed.	Either	Full sun; partial shade in very hot climates	Water well until established and then provide regular water.	Once a month during harvest time.	30 days from start; 75–85 days from seed. Snip stems at base of plant, but don't cut more than ⅓ of the plant at once.
Cilantro	1 gallon (5 L) or larger; best if 12" (30 cm) deep	In spring after frost danger has passed— succession plant every 2 weeks.	Seed	Full sun to partial shade; afternoon shade in hot climates.	Water well until established and then provide regular water. Don't get water on leaves.	Half-strength fertilizer every 2 weeks.	21–28 days. Harvest by cutting stalks at soil level.
Dill	3 gallon (14 L) or larger, at least 12" (30 cm) deep	In spring after frost danger has passed— succession plant every 3 weeks.	Seed	Full sun	Water well until established and then let the top inch (2.5 cm) of soil dry out between watering.	Not usually necessary.	60–70 days. Harvest fronds when they've reached 6" (15 cm) tall or higher, just before the plant flowers.

PLANT	CONTAINER SIZE	WHEN TO PLANT	SEED OR START	SUN	WATER	FERTILIZER	HARVEST
Lemongrass	5 gallon (23 L) or larger	Late spring or summer	Start	Full sun	Water well until established and then provide regular water.	Every 2 weeks during growing season.	Cut mature stems when about the thickness of a pencil.
Marjoram	1 gallon (5 L) or larger	In spring after frost danger has passed.	Start	Full sun	Water well until established and then let the top inch (2.5 cm) of soil dry out between watering.	Once or twice during the growing season.	4–6 weeks after transplant. Pick leaves as needed.
Mint	3 gallon (14 L) or larger	In spring after frost danger has passed.	Start	Partial shade	Water well until established and then provide regular water.	At beginning of the season.	30 days. Pick leaves as needed but never more than ⅓ of the plant at one time.
Oregano	3 gallon (14 L) or larger	In spring after frost danger has passed.	Start	Full sun; partial shade in very hot climates.	Water well until established and then let the top inch (2.5 cm) of soil dry out between watering.	At beginning of the season.	30 days. Pick leaves as needed but never more than ⅓ of the plant at one time.
Parsley	2 gallon (9 L) or larger, 12" (30 cm) deep is best	5 weeks before last spring frost.	Start	Full sun to partial shade	Water well until established and then provide regular water.	Once or twice during the growing season.	30 days. Harvest individual stems as needed.
Rosemary	3 gallon (14 L) or larger	In spring after frost danger has passed.	Start	Full sun	Keep soil barely moist until established and then water occasionally.	Once or twice during the growing season.	Cut the fresh growth with scissors or pruners; don't take more than ⅓ of the plant at one time.

PLANT	CONTAINER SIZE	WHEN TO PLANT	SEED OR START	SUN	WATER	FERTILIZER	HARVEST
Sage	2 gallon (9 L) or larger	In spring after frost danger has passed.	Start	Full sun	Water well until established and then let the top inch (2.5 cm) of soil dry out between watering.	Once or twice during the growing season.	Cut leaves just before the plant flowers.
Tarragon	1 gallon (5 L) or larger	In spring after frost danger has passed.	Start	Full sun to partial shade	Keep soil moist until established, and then let the top inch (2.5 cm) of soil dry out between watering.	Once or twice during the growing season.	Snip top leaves in early summer.
Thyme	1 gallon (5 L) or larger	2–3 weeks after last spring frost.	Start	Full sun with afternoon shade in hot climates.	Keep soil barely moist until established and then water occasionally.	Once or twice during the growing season.	Cut stems just before the plant flowers; don't take more than ¼ of the plant at one time.

The 10 Best Container Vegetable Plants

Overwhelmed by all the choices? The following 10 vegetables are a great place for first-time container vegetable gardeners to start.

Bush Bean

Bush beans have large seeds, making them easy for kids to plant. All bush beans work well in containers because of their small size. Look for compact types if you have limited space; standard-size bush beans can grow up to 2 feet (60 cm) tall.

- Warm season
- 'Compass' filet bean
- 'Mascotte' snap bean
- 'Gold Rush' yellow wax bean

Bonus tip: Succession plant beans every 2–3 weeks to ensure a continuous harvest.

Chard

Chard thrives in containers, and many types have beautiful, colored stems. Add chard to a container with flowers for a stunning showpiece in the front yard garden.

- Warm and cool seasons
- 'Apple Blossom Blend'
- 'Rainbow'

Bonus tip: Harvest when 2–4 inches (5–10 cm) tall and eat as baby greens or allow plant to grow to full size.

Cucumber

Cucumbers are easy to care for, and one plant will produce a bumper crop. Try a unique variety like 'Heirloom Lemon' along with the traditional supermarket variety.

- Warm season
- 'Spacemaster 80' slicer
- 'Tasty Green' burpless
- 'Heirloom Lemon' slicer

Bonus tip: Most cucumbers are vines and need a trellis or stake for support, although there are a few bush varieties. Don't let the soil dry out, or the cucumbers will be bitter and hollow.

Eggplant

Eggplants like hot weather and thrive in dark-colored containers that retain heat. Different varieties produce purple, white, or green fruit.

- Warm season
- 'Long Purple'
- 'Fairy Tale'
- 'Bambino'

Bonus tip: Use a stake to support the plant later in the season. This will protect it from breaking as the fruits get large and heavy.

Kale

Kale is a versatile green, and it looks beautiful in containers even if you don't want to eat it (I won't tell). Look for varieties with "dwarf" in the name—some types of kale grow up to 5 feet (1.5 m) tall.

- Cool season
- 'Dwarf Blue Curled Vates'
- 'Dwarf Siberian'

Bonus tip: Harvest kale often by removing just a few lower leaves at a time. By leaving the growing point intact, the plant will continue to produce new leaves.

Lettuce

There's no better feeling than heading out to the garden and picking your own salad for dinner. Head lettuces and mesclun blends alike are great for containers.

- Cool season
- 'Little Gem' romaine
- 'Marvel of Four Seasons' butterhead
- 'Great Lakes 118' iceberg

Bonus tip: Lettuce has shallow roots, so don't let the soil dry out.

Peas

Fresh peas are several thousand times better than the canned ones we ate as kids. You'll probably find yourself munching on these as fast as you can pick them.

- Cool season
- 'Oregon Sugar Pod II' snow pea
- 'Green Arrow' shelling pea
- 'Sugar Snap' snap pea
- 'Tom Thumb' shelling pea

Bonus tip: Most peas are vines and will need a trellis or stakes for support.

Pepper

Even though container peppers are compact, they produce like crazy. In a warm climate, peppers sometimes survive the winter and produce for a second year.

- Warm season
- 'Bull Nose Bell' sweet
- 'Baby Belle' sweet
- 'Mirasol' hot

Bonus tip: Water peppers thoroughly, and harvest often to encourage production.

Summer Squash

There are many colorful types of summer squash, and their large seeds are easy for kids to plant. Compact bush varieties work best in containers.

- Warm season
- 'Astia' zucchini
- 'Golden Star' golden zucchini
- 'Dwarf Summer' crookneck
- 'Sunburst' pattypan

Bonus tip: Harvest every couple of days when the squash are small. They will grow from a normal size to gigantic seemingly overnight.

Tomato

Homegrown tomatoes are a summer classic, and there are many types that thrive in containers. It's fun to sit on the patio on a summer evening and munch cherry tomatoes right off the vine.

- Warm season
- 'Beaverlodge' plum
- 'Little Napoli' plum
- 'Early Girl Bush' slicer
- 'Tiny Tim' cherry

Bonus tip: Plum or slicer tomatoes will need a cage or trellis; cherry tomato plants typically stay small. Use a large, deep container and water consistently to prevent blossom end rot.

Companion plants

As you're designing your container garden, consider combining multiple plants in a larger container. This is a great way to maximize your planting space. Most of the time, it's fine to plant different vegetables or fruits in the same container—provided that it's large enough, of course.

Did you know that (just like people), some plants get along better than others? Plants that grow well together are called *companion plants*, and plants that don't are called *repellent plants*. Companion plants keep bugs away, and help neighboring plants grow better. Repellent plants can prevent each other from growing well, so they need to be kept apart.

There are entire books written about companion and repellent plants, this chart will give you a quick overview for the plants in this book.

Companion and Repellant Plants for Container Vegetables

VEGETABLE	COMPANION	REPELLENT
Bush Bean	Cucumber, strawberry, potato, rosemary	Onion
Beet	Onion	
Cucumber	Bush bean, pea, radish	Potato, sage
Eggplant	Bush bean, potato	
Garlic	Raspberry	Bush bean, pea
Kale	Dill, sage, rosemary	Strawberry, tomato
Lettuce	Radish, strawberry, cucumber, onion	
Melon	Okra	Potato
Pea	Radish, cucumber, bush bean	Onion, garlic, potato, chives
Pepper (sweet or hot)	Basil, okra	
Potato	Bush bean, eggplant	Summer squash, cucumber, tomato, raspberry
Radish	Pea, lettuce, cucumber	
Rosemary	Bush bean, sage	
Sage	Rosemary	Cucumber
Spinach	Strawberry	
Strawberry	Bush bean, spinach, lettuce, onion	Cabbage
Tomato	Basil, chives, parsley	Potato

Table sources: *Plant Partners: Science-Based Companion Planting Strategies for the Vegetable Garden* by Jessica Walliser; *Carrots Love Tomatoes: Secrets of Companion Planting for Successful Gardening* by Louise Riotte; *How to Grow More Vegetables (and Fruits, Nuts, Berries, Grains, and Other Crops) Than You Ever Thought Possible on Less Land Than You Can Imagine* by John Jeavons.

This colorful jumble of nasturtium, tomatoes, thyme, and mint are companion plants that help each other grow.

Why Container Size Matters

Choosing the correct container size is one of the biggest keys to success with container vegetable growing. Always opt for the largest pot you can afford and fit in the given space. A larger soil volume means your plants' roots will have plenty of room to grow and support big yields and a healthy plant. Plus, you'll have to water less frequently. In the next chapter, we'll take a look at some different options for containers and how to choose the best one for whatever you want to grow. But first, let me share some of my favorite container vegetable planting combinations to get you started.

Be sure to choose a container that's big enough for the mature plant (and for a curious little puppy).

Planting Recipes

Container Combinations

You might be thinking, "Holy moly, this gardening business sounds pretty complicated! Plants and containers and soil—it's all too much." It's easy to feel that way when you're a new gardener, and that's why I've created these container combination gardens to help get you started.

Each of the planting plans that follows contains plants that grow well together and have similar sun, water, and fertilizer needs. These vegetables, fruits, and herbs will happily coexist, and the illustrations give you a peek into the future of your garden. Pretty cool, right?

Your container can be any shape or material you'd like (check Chapter 3 for information on container materials). If you can't find a planter that's big enough, use several smaller ones. And if your container is larger than the size indicated, you can add more plants or spread them out, so they have more room to grow.

Don't like one of the plants in a specific combination? No problem—it's okay to leave it out. Replace it with more of the other plants in the combo or add some flowers to attract pollinators. Sweet alyssum and nasturtium are great choices, and they'll drape beautifully over the edge of your planter.

Let's get your garden started.

Windowsill Herb Garden

A windowsill herb garden is a great way to start container gardening. It's also a wonderful housewarming gift and a unique host gift. If you're combining multiple herbs in one pot, choose a larger container that's at least 4 inches (10 cm) deep. For a grouping of containers, several ¼-gallon (1 L) pots are ideal. Place your garden in a south- or southwest-facing window if you can, for maximum sunlight. Snip leaves off as needed, but don't take more than ⅓ of the plant when you harvest. If you cut off the green onions just above the soil level, they will regrow in a few weeks.

CONTAINER SIZE: 2 gallon (9 L)

LOCATION: Bright, sunny window

FERTILIZER: When planting and two months after

PLANTS:

- 6 green onions
- 1 purple basil
- 1 green basil
- 1 parsley
- 1 oregano

Smoothie Greens

Green smoothies are a great way to get the day started. They're packed full of nutrition and are an easy way to get lots of fiber and vitamins while you're on the go. It's easy to grow the greens for your smoothie and save lots of money while you're at it. When you're shopping for seeds or plants, look for varieties that are mild in flavor. You can harvest all of these by the "cut and come again" method, which means you pick a few leaves from the outside of the plant. The rest of the plant will continue growing so you have a nearly endless supply of smoothie ingredients.

CONTAINER SIZE: 7 gallon (32 L)

LOCATION: Full sun/partial shade

FERTILIZER: When planting and three months after

PLANTS:

- 6 spinach
- 2 kale
- 2 chard
- 1 dandelion

Salsa

When you grow your own vegetables, you can customize your salsa recipe. Make it as spicy or mild as you like, with the peppers you choose. Add lots of onions, leave out the cilantro—it's all good. Be sure to choose a plum or paste tomato, which are meaty and less watery than traditional slicing tomatoes. Plant the garlic in the fall and plant the other salsa ingredients in the spring.

CONTAINER SIZE: 20 gallon (91 L)

LOCATION: Full sun

FERTILIZER: Every two weeks

PLANTS:

- 1 garlic
- 1 plum or paste tomato
- 1 pepper (sweet or hot)
- 6 green onions
- 4 cilantro

Deluxe Herb Garden

Although these pots with cutout sides are designed for strawberries, they're also perfect for an all-in-one herb garden. Mix and match any sturdy herbs you like with similar sun and water needs. (Delicate herbs like cilantro and jumbo plants like dill won't do well here.) Plant chives in the top, and one plant in each cutout space. Add some small flowers like violas for extra pizazz.

CONTAINER: Strawberry jar

LOCATION: Full sun

FERTILIZER: When planting and two months after

PLANTS:

- 2 chives
- 1 rosemary
- 1 basil
- 1 parsley
- 1 marjoram
- 1 oregano
- 1 sage

Kids' Garden

Kids who grow vegetables love to eat vegetables, and these are all easy to grow and snack on right off the vine.

Put a trellis or small support on one side for the purple snow peas. Plant a red or yellow cherry tomato next to it, with strawberries and a minipumpkin in the front. The minipumpkin vine will cascade over the edge of the container as it grows. As the season continues, pull the snow peas out and replace them with Persian minicucumbers.

CONTAINER SIZE: 10 gallon (45 L)

LOCATION: Full sun

FERTILIZER: Every two weeks

PLANTS:

- 4 purple snow peas
- 1 red or yellow cherry tomato
- 4 strawberries
- 1 minipumpkin
- 2 Persian minicucumber

Fruit Basket

There are so many possibilities with a fruit basket garden—these are our family's favorites. If you don't like apples, substitute any dwarf fruit tree you like. Some growers offer grafted fruit trees that have different varieties on the same tree! Plant the tree slightly toward the back of the container, allowing it and the raspberry room to grow. Tuck the strawberries and cantaloupe or watermelon in the front, so the melon vine can grow over the edge of the container. You'll replant the melon each year, but the other fruits are perennials and will grow and fruit for many years.

CONTAINER SIZE: 30 gallon (136 L)

LOCATION: Full sun

FERTILIZER: Monthly during growing season

PLANTS:

- 1 cantaloupe or watermelon
- 1 dwarf apple tree
- 1 bush raspberry
- 6–10 strawberries

Spring Stir-Fry

Plant these vegetables in winter for your spring stir-fry. It might seem strange to start a garden in the winter, but these vegetables don't mind the cold. You'll quickly have enough vegetables for an early spring stir-fry, plus some snap peas to munch on while you cook. Put a trellis at the back for the snap peas and plant the chard and baby spinach in the front. If you cut off the green onions just above the soil level, they will regrow in a few weeks. Continue your stir-fry garden after the snap peas die off by planting one or two bush beans.

CONTAINER SIZE: 15 gallon (68 L)

LOCATION: Full sun/partial shade

FERTILIZER: When planting and two months after

PLANTS:

- 4 snap peas
- 2 chard
- 4 baby spinach
- 6 green onions
- 2 bush beans

Salad

What kind of salad is your favorite? You can grow spinach, lettuce, leafy greens, or baby kale in your salad garden. Most of these can be continually harvested—pick the outer leaves and allow the inner ones to continue growing. This is called "cut and come again" harvesting. Place a trellis at the back for the cucumber and add the other vegetables once the cucumber is big enough to provide some shade. Succession plant the radishes and green onions to ensure a continuous harvest.

CONTAINER SIZE: 10 gallon (45 L)

LOCATION: Full sun/partial shade

FERTILIZER: Monthly

PLANTS:

- 4 spinach/baby kale or 2 lettuce
- 1 cucumber
- 6 radish
- 6 green onions

Spaghetti Sauce

These vegetables and herbs are great in many different recipes, but together they form the basis of a delicious spaghetti sauce. Choose a plum or paste tomato, which have fewer seeds than traditional slicing tomatoes. If you're growing other vegetables, you can shred them and add them in your spaghetti sauce for extra nutrition. Plant the garlic in the fall and add the other plants in the spring.

CONTAINER SIZE: 20 gallon (91 L)

LOCATION: Full sun

FERTILIZER: When planting and every two weeks thereafter

PLANTS:

- 1 garlic
- 1 plum or paste tomato
- 1 sweet pepper
- 4 basil
- 2 oregano

Adorable Minis

If nothing in the world is cool enough for your tween daughter, this might just change her mind. This garden of adorable miniature vegetables is easy to grow and is a prolific producer throughout the summer and fall. Grow the Persian cucumber and cucamelon on a trellis with the multicolored baby bell pepper in front. The minipumpkin and 'Eight Ball' zucchini can hang over the edge of the container.

CONTAINER SIZE: 20 gallon (91 L)

LOCATION: Full sun

FERTILIZER: Monthly

PLANTS:

- 1 Persian cucumber
- 1 cucamelon
- 1 baby bell pepper
- 1 minipumpkin
- 1 'Eight Ball' zucchini

Rainbow Vegetables

This is the real way to taste the rainbow, unlike those candies that use the term in their ads. This colorful combination of vegetables and alyssum flowers is beautiful and versatile in the kitchen. Eggplant, chard, and peppers are great in stir-fry, and mature chard leaves are perfect for lettuce wraps. The fragrant alyssum blossoms attract pollinators and drape beautifully over the edge of the container. Plant the chard at the back of the container, with the peppers and eggplant in front of them. Tuck the alyssum flowers along the front of the container so they'll hang over the edge as they grow.

CONTAINER SIZE: 30 gallon (136 L)

LOCATION: Full sun

FERTILIZER: When planting and monthly thereafter

PLANTS:

- 2 'Rainbow' chard
- 2 baby bell peppers
- 2 variegated eggplant
- 4 white alyssum

Cocktail or Mocktail

An icy-cold drink is just what you need at the end of a long day in the garden. These herbs and fruits are wonderful for lemonade, mojitos, margaritas, or smoothies. Plant the lemon tree in the center and cluster the herbs and strawberries in sections around it. Mint tends to take over a container, so be ruthless and pull any extra plants that sprout up. Cheers!

CONTAINER SIZE: 30 gallon (136 L)

LOCATION: Full sun

FERTILIZER: Monthly

PLANTS:

• 1 Meyer lemon tree
• 6 strawberries
• 2 mint
• 4 basil
• 4 thyme

Creating a lush and productive container vegetable garden requires the right veggies, the right pots, the right soil, and care from you!

3

Choose Your Containers

When we started our first garden as newly-weds, we were on a tight budget. We used hand-me-down planters and recycled buckets for growing vegetables and watered them with the hose after we got home from work. No fancy containers or automatic sprinklers for us. We were more concerned with supplementing our tiny food budget than with the look of our garden!

Some plants did well in those makeshift pots, and some didn't. We had lots and lots of cucumbers and green beans, but the tomatoes didn't do well at all. The next year we used a larger pot for our tomatoes, and they were much happier. None of those freebie pots were big enough for fruit trees or berries, so that part of our garden had to wait.

Today our garden is full of large half-barrel planters, fabric grow bags, and colorful pots, with all kinds of vegetables, fruit, herbs, and flowers growing in them. Over the years, we've added containers and sprinklers as our budget allowed.

One of the most fun aspects of container gardening is choosing containers that fit your aesthetic. You can get modern, sleek, concrete planters; rustic wood half-barrels; colorful plastic pots; and so much more. Better yet, you can recycle and upcycle existing containers to personalize your garden and save money. No matter what size of container you find or buy, there is something you can grow. Over the years, I've grown garlic in an old wheelbarrow, strawberries in a laundry basket, and parsley in a soup can on my windowsill.

When you're choosing containers, just remember **BFG**. Your garden pots, whatever they're made from, need to be

Big enough: choose a container that's large enough for the mature plant. Most of the time, the plant tag or seed packet will tell you how big the plant will be. When in doubt, it's better to choose a larger container instead of a smaller one.

Food safe: choose containers that are designed for growing food. If you're upcycling or recycling containers, avoid containers that held chemicals or were made from unsafe materials. If you wouldn't eat out of it, don't grow in it.

Good drainage: most food plants need regular water, but don't want to sit in soggy soil. Drain holes in your containers are a must. Many purchased pots will have drain holes; if your container of choice doesn't have drain holes, you'll need to add them.

Big Enough: Container Size

Once you've decided on the vegetables, fruits, and herbs you want to grow, it's time to choose the right container to grow them in. A container that's the correct size will ensure that the plant and its roots have plenty of room to grow and thrive. When a plant's roots can spread out and access water and the nutrients in soil, the plant will be healthier and more productive.

Container size is expressed in inches, centimeters, gallons, or liters. When you see a pot measured in inches or centimeters, that's the distance across the top opening. A measurement in gallons or liters indicates how much soil is needed to fill the container. Which brings us to . . .

Lettuce, strawberries, and peas thrive in this tiered basket organizer. By planting in this unique hanging container, these tender plants are less likely to be eaten by snails and slugs.

Whether you're using purchased or upcycled containers, ensure that they are big enough for the mature plant, made of food safe material, and have good drainage.

HOW MUCH SOIL?

Containers measured in inches (centimeters) don't always indicate how much soil they will hold. And just to be confusing, most potting soil is sold in bags measured by the quart. See Chapter 4 for more information on the best kind of soil for your container garden.

This chart translates between standard nursery container sizes and soil packages.

CONTAINER SOIL VOLUMES		
Container Diameter Size in Inches/Centimeters	Equivalent Container Size in Gallons/Liters	Soil Needed in
6" (15 cm)	¼ gallon (1 L)	1 quart (1 L)
8" (20 cm)	1 gallon (5 L)	4 quarts (5 L)
10" (25 cm)	3 gallons (14 L)	12 quarts (14 L)
12" (30 cm)	5 gallons (23 L)	20 quarts (23 L)
14" (36 cm)	7 gallons (32 L)	28 quarts (32 L)
16" (41 cm)	10 gallons (45 L)	40 quarts (45 L)
18" (46 cm)	15 gallons (68 L)	60 quarts (68 L)
24" (60 cm)	25 gallons (114 L)	100 quarts (114 L)
30" (76 cm)	30 gallons (136 L)	120 quarts (136 L)

We got a few tomatoes from our first garden, but the containers were too small to allow the plants to produce fully.

Radishes don't require much room and are a quick and simple crop to grow in spring.

CHOOSING A CONTAINER

When selecting a container, think about the root depth and size of the plant when it's fully grown. You'll match the container size to the plant that's growing in it. A citrus tree needs a much bigger pot than radishes, for example.

Refer to the chart on pages 42–44 to see the best container sizes for specific plants. If you plan to combine several plants together into a single pot, add all of their soil volume needs together to determine how big of a pot you need for all of them in. Remember **BFG**, and keep these tips in mind:

- In general, a deep container is better than a wide, shallow container. This is because a deep container retains water better, and the deep soil gives the roots more room to grow and access nutrients.

- Most fruit-producing trees and shrubs are perennials and require a bigger container to support their larger root systems.

- Root vegetables, like carrots, beets, and potatoes, need a deeper container than vegetables that grow above ground.

- Large plants, like tomatoes and pumpkins, have extensive root systems and need big containers. Tomatoes may also need a cage or other support to keep them upright.

- If you plant in a container that's too small, your plant won't automatically die. It just won't grow as well as it could or provide as much food as it could in optimal conditions.

RIGHT: The right size container is essential for your plants to grow and thrive. A fruit tree requires a much bigger pot than a crop of radishes.

Food-Safe Container Materials

Whether you're buying new or recycling containers, there are lots and lots of materials to choose from. You always want to choose planters that are food safe—which is especially important when using recycled containers. The utility buckets at the hardware store and buckets that held swimming pool chlorine are not safe for planting. Containers that were designed for food, like milk jugs and large soup cans, are safe. And of course, the planters at the garden center are fine for growing food.

The fun part about container gardening is showing off your sense of style with your containers. Your garden will do just fine in a rustic wood planter, upcycled bucket, or a sleek, ceramic pot. There isn't a "wrong" container material for a particular plant.

Upcycling containers is a great way to garden on a budget. This parsley and sage are happily growing in soup cans on the windowsill.

How about recycling old recycling containers to make a garden? Just be sure there are drainage holes in the bottom.

While there are many, many types of planter materials, the easiest way to categorize them is by porosity. Porous containers allow water and air to move more easily through them; nonporous containers do not. Both types have advantages and disadvantages, and you'll quickly adapt to whichever kind of planter material you choose.

Here are the most popular types of container materials and the pros/cons of each.

POROUS

Unglazed Clay/Terra-cotta

These are the ubiquitous dark orange containers that are in every plant store. They're inexpensive, come in many shapes and sizes, and are easily painted or otherwise decorated.

Pros: easy to find, with a neutral, classic look that's available in many sizes.

Cons: heavy, especially in larger sizes; prone to breaking if dropped. Can get salt, lime, or moss stained over time. Because they're porous and absorb water, they can crack during freezing temperatures.

Unglazed Clay/Terra-cotta

Fabric

You might be surprised to learn that you can garden in fabric containers! Varieties include grow bags, upcycled jeans, reusable grocery bags, and some fabric hanging baskets.

Pros: fold flat for storage, lightweight, and affordable. Drains well, keeps plants from being rootbound. Place inside a decorative pot (cachepot) for an improved aesthetic.

Cons: available in limited sizes and colors. Not suitable for permanent plantings. Lower-quality and upcycled fabric containers will degrade within a year or two.

Fabric

Wood

Wood containers may be purpose-built or recycled—the half-barrel planter is a classic example. Other wood planters are made from wine crates and boxes, pallets, or hollowed-out tree stumps.

Pros: the wood half-barrel is one of the most common materials for container gardening. Wood is relatively inexpensive and if it hasn't been painted or chemically treated, it's safe for growing food.

Cons: most wood breaks down after several years, especially if exposed to a lot of water. If a wood container sits directly on the soil, the bottom is likely to rot out.

Wood

Concrete or Stone

Concrete or Stone

Planting in concrete is easier than you might think. As long as the container has drainage, it will be a great planter. You can upcycle an old bird bath, plant herbs in cinder blocks, and much more.

Pros: stone and concrete are durable, with a modern aesthetic. They provide good insulation for delicate roots.

Cons: both of these materials are heavy—if using a larger container, place it in an area that can handle the weight. There's a chance the soil could expand in freezing temperatures and crack the pot. It can be tricky to add extra drainage holes to these containers.

NONPOROUS

Plastic

Plastic containers are easy to find and they're an economical way to start your garden. Examples of plastic pots include buckets, bowls, planters, milk jugs, and takeout containers.

Pros: lightweight, affordable, and available in a variety of sizes and colors. Easy to sterilize if you're recycling or upcycling. Best choice for a kids' garden because of their durability.

Cons: some containers are more durable than others; all can become brittle and crack over time.

Metal

Metal containers can be fun for planting—imagine lettuce planted in an old colander, or a red wagon or wheelbarrow full of vegetables. Most metal is quite thin and temperature extremes can damage plant roots, though.

Pros: metal containers are relatively inexpensive and easy to find. They're easy to paint or customize, and won't chip, crack, or break.

Cons: most don't come with drain holes, and some metal containers will rust or dent. Metal planters will transfer heat and cold to the plant's roots, so there is a danger that the plant will freeze in the cold or cook in the heat.

Plastic

Metal

FIBERGLASS

These containers are made of thin fibers of spun glass held together by resin, and they're molded into many unique colors and shapes.

Pros: lightweight, rustproof, and weatherproof. Fiberglass planters are made in modern, traditional, and rustic designs.

Cons: tall, narrow fiberglass planters could be too light-weight for heavier plants and may tip over, especially in windy conditions. Fiberglass traps heat and can cook plant roots.

GLAZED CERAMIC

The large, striking containers you see outside stores and restaurants are usually glazed ceramic. They are durable and long lasting.

Pros: available in many sizes, shapes, and colors, with unusual glazes and patterns. They're heavy, which is good for windy areas. The material is fairly thick, which helps insulate roots from extreme heat and cold.

Cons: can be very expensive and heavy. Freezing weather could cause soil to expand and crack the container. It's hard to add drain holes to these pots.

Fiberglass

Can plants get too big for their containers?

Yes, plants can outgrow their containers. You can tell if a plant has outgrown its pot if there are roots coming out through the drain holes, or if the roots are growing around and around inside the confines of the pot.

If an annual vegetable or herb has outgrown its pot near the end of the growing season, pull the plant and add it to your compost bin. If it's the beginning of the season or if the plant is a perennial, it's best to transplant it into a larger container. It won't automatically die if it stays in the smaller container, but it will grow slowly and produce less food than it would in an ideal situation.

Glazed Ceramic

A broken wheelbarrow can be easily repurposed into a planter with the addition of good soil and a few drain holes.

RECYCLING/REPURPOSING CONTAINERS

Recycling, or upcycling, is a great way to get your garden started. There are so many creative items you can plant in, and many times you can get them cheaply or for free. You might find yourself searching the thrift store for that perfect, unique garden piece—and finding it!

Here are some free or inexpensive container ideas:

- Large buckets from the grocery store bakery
- Industrial-size food tins
- Milk jugs or plastic soda bottles
- Plastic take-out containers from restaurants
- Wooden wine boxes

Not sure what to plant in your upcycled containers? Here's some planting inspiration:

- Herbs in an empty rotisserie chicken container
- Lettuce in an old colander
- Strawberries in a laundry basket
- Herbs in a pretty teacup and saucer

Containers to avoid

Planting in unique and recycled containers is a great idea! However, some of these planters are not food safe. These items could leach chemicals into the soil, and possibly your food. It is best to avoid using

- Old tires
- Pressure-treated wood
- Wood that is stained, painted, or sealed
- Plastic buckets that aren't food safe
- Antiques that may contain lead paint or asbestos

If you have your heart set on a container that's on the danger list, all is not lost. Use that container as a cachepot and put the plant-safe container inside of it.

Good Drainage: Container Considerations

For plant health and good root development, the soil must drain properly and have space for air. Soil that is too heavy or dense can slow drainage (see Chapter 4 for soil recommendations). Also watch for containers with blocked drain holes or no drain holes at all.

Good drainage makes the difference between a healthy plant and one with rotted roots. Container plants are much more likely to die from drowning or root rot than from under watering.

You're less likely to have drainage problems with containers made of porous materials, because their very nature encourages drainage and water evaporation. If you're using nonporous containers, you must add drain holes.

Disinfecting Containers

It's important to disinfect reused or upcycled containers before planting in them. This helps prevent any dirt, diseases, or insect eggs from damaging your new plants. Empty the container and rinse or brush off any soil or debris on the inside or outside.

Grab a bucket, gloves, and eye protection. Make a bleach solution with bleach that contains 5–9% sodium hypochlorite (don't use splashless bleach, which isn't strong enough to disinfect). Add ¼ cup (60 mL) of bleach for every gallon (3.8 L) of water. Soak the containers in this solution for at least 1 minute before removing them and rinsing them thoroughly.

If you're planting in a container that's hard to disinfect, like a large wood or ceramic container, consider lining it with plastic to keep your plants safe. Remember to add drain holes!

ADDING DRAIN HOLES TO A CONTAINER

If you're using a container that doesn't have drain holes, you can easily add them. This is especially helpful for large plastic buckets, wooden half-barrels, and recycled/upcycled containers. Here's how.

1 Assemble your materials: container, safety glasses, electric drill, and ½" (12.7 mm) drill bit. For unglazed ceramics like terra-cotta, use a masonry bit. Glazed ceramics require a diamond-tipped bit. These can be tricky to drill through without cracking, though. Use a metal bit for metal containers, and drill through very slowly. Place the container upside-down on a flat, stable surface to drill the drainage holes.

2 Decide where you want the drain holes to be and mark the spots with a pencil or marker. On a large container like this, I put two holes in the middle and several around the perimeter. Evenly space the drain holes from each other and from the edge of the container. Putting holes too close together can weaken the base of the container.

3 Hold the drill perpendicular to the base. You can make a perfectly straight hole by using a piece of scrap wood as a guide, to ensure you drill straight down.

4 Drill slowly, applying a bit of pressure. If the drill jams or stops partway through, release the trigger. Pull the bit out of the hole and start the drill before putting the bit back in the hole. Push straight down until the bit goes through the material. When through, pull the drill straight out until the bit is completely out of the hole.

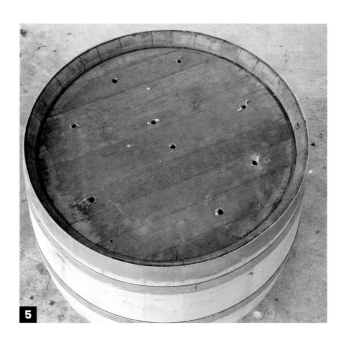

5 Repeat until all the holes are drilled. Sometimes the drain holes will have rough bits or splinters around the edge, and that's ok. Now your container is ready to fill with soil.

Water isn't draining

The most common reason that your container isn't draining properly is because soil or roots have clogged up the drain holes. To fix this, tip the pot carefully on its side and poke the drain holes with a pencil or screwdriver to loosen the soil. If you've chosen potting soil that's labeled "moisture control," it has small polymer crystals that absorb lots of water (sort of like the stuff in disposable diapers). After these crystals soak up lots of water, they don't release it properly to the plant, so using moisture-control additives in container soil isn't a good choice for growing your food plants.

If your pot fills with water and doesn't drain, the holes in the bottom of the container may be filled with roots or debris.

SOIL LOSS THROUGH DRAIN HOLES

If you're worried about soil spilling out through the drain holes, there are several ways to prevent this. My favorites are to lay a coffee filter or a single sheet of newspaper in the bottom of the pot before the soil is added. These materials are biodegradable and will keep the loose soil from leaking out.

Some people staple a bit of mesh or a piece of window screen over the holes, but I don't recommend that. Those materials aren't biodegradable, and sometimes you need to loosen the soil by pushing a pencil or screwdriver up through the drainage hole (see Water Isn't Draining, above). If there's a permanent screen in place, you can't do that.

The big drainage myth

There's a long-standing garden myth that says you should add "filler material" to the bottom of your container to make it lighter and improve soil drainage. This myth has been put to the test and it is **busted**. Please do not add empty bottles, cans, packing peanuts, very small rocks, broken pot shards, or anything but soil to your container.

Adding filler to your container is harmful in several ways:

- It reduces the amount of soil that plants have for their roots to absorb nutrients.
- It changes the center of gravity, making it easier for the pot to fall over.
- Water doesn't easily pass from the denser soil to the looser filler material because the materials have different porosity. This means the water collects in the soil, potentially drowning your plants—which is exactly what you're trying to avoid!

Worried about moving a heavy container? Don't use filler to make the container lighter. Use casters or a plant caddy instead.

CONTAINER ACCESSORIES FOR DRAINAGE AND MOBILITY

Once you've made sure your container has adequate drainage, ensure the drain holes can do their job. Don't set a container with a smooth base directly on a deck or flat surface because doing so can prevent water from draining. The water that drains out carries minerals and sometimes a bit of soil with it, and this water can damage a wood deck or stain a concrete deck.

Here are a few of the accessories you can use to help with container drainage and mobility.

Pot Feet or Pot Toes

Pot feet and pot toes are small lifts, usually made of clay or plastic, that keep a container from sitting directly on a flat surface. They can be plain or decorative and allow containers to drain fully. This reduces water stains on surfaces, keeps plants from getting root rot, and helps prevent bugs from hatching and living under the container. You can also make your own lifts with bricks, scraps of wood, or even sturdy plastic bottle caps.

Pot Feet or Pot Toes

Saucers and Drip Trays

Saucers and Drip Trays

Plant saucers and drip trays sit under the planter to collect excess water that has drained out. Saucers prevent this water from staining or rotting the surface under your plants. They can be attached to the planter or purchased separately. Be sure to empty the saucer after watering because the roots can drown if water is held in the saucer. Upcycled shallow bowls or plastic plates are an economical option.

Plant Caddy

A plant caddy is like a tiny furniture dolly—a wheeled platform that holds the pot off the ground and makes it easy to move. If you're growing fruit trees or bushes in containers and need to move them inside for the winter, a plant caddy is the way to go. The container of herbs shown here can easily be moved from one sunny spot to another with the plant caddy.

RIGHT: Plant Caddy

WINTERIZING YOUR CONTAINERS

Because container soil retains water, the soil can freeze and expand during cold weather. This can result in containers cracking and even breaking apart—which is an expensive problem if you've purchased larger pots. This problem is avoidable with a little preparation. Before filling the container with soil, line the sides of the pot (not quite all the way to the top) with two layers of bubble wrap. Be sure not to block any drain holes. The bubble wrap provides insulation for the soil and plant roots and a cushioning layer when the soil water expands after freezing. The bubble wrap won't be visible when the container is filled with soil.

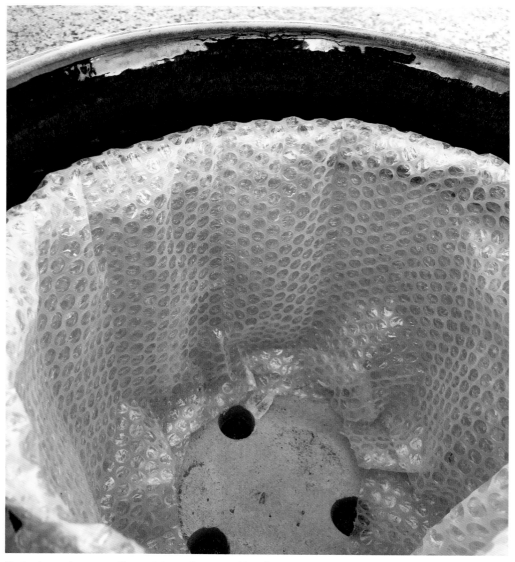

Protect your large, costly containers from cracking due to soil moisture expansion when it freezes in the winter. Line the inside with a bit of bubble wrap, which provides insulation and flexibility.

Container Aesthetics

For most food plants, the shape and material of a container is not as important as its soil capacity and depth. For example: carrots will grow just as well in a square clay pot or a round metal container, as long as the container is deep enough.

If you have a particular aesthetic in mind for your garden, here are some ideas to help you get started.

CYLINDRICAL CONTAINERS

Half-barrels, round pots, vase or urn shapes

- Look great when placed together, especially in corners or spirals.

- Use one large container as a focal point in the yard or garden.

- More natural or rustic looking; best suited for a traditional garden.

SQUARE CONTAINERS

Upcycled metal, wood boxes, stone, or resin

- If placed in a group or along a border, must be lined up carefully.

- Striking as a stand-alone feature in the garden.

- Modern and minimalist; best suited for a formal garden.

RECTANGULAR CONTAINERS

Troughs, window boxes, or elevated planters

- Great for creating a border or placing at the bottom of a wall.

- Can sit on top of other surfaces (windowsill, porch railing) if secured properly.

- Depending on material, can be used in a traditional or formal garden.

Cylindrical Containers

Square Containers

This rooftop garden spans the seasons. The broccoli is ready to harvest and the tomatoes are just getting started.

What you fill your pot with—well before you
add the plants—is essential for a productive
container garden.

4

Container Gardening Soil

Contrary to what you might think, I haven't always been good at growing food. Our kids have helped in the garden since they were tiny, and we've learned something new every growing season. Sometimes we have bumper crops of vegetables, and other times we have complete failures (the carefully nurtured russet potatoes that grew to the size of golf balls are a good example). Part of being a gardener is always being willing to learn, adapt, and try again next year.

When I started my website, my dad asked me why I named it "Brown Thumb Mama" instead of Green Thumb. I reminded him of my previous summer in the garden. I had carefully started my zucchini seeds indoors, acclimated them to the outdoors slowly, and transplanted them at the beginning of the season. And what happened? Absolutely nothing. They grew a little bit, but never flowered or set fruit. The kids planted green beans, and they too were a complete bust. So, I decided that it was more realistic to declare that I had a "brown thumb"—sometimes my vegetables grew well, and sometimes they didn't.

But what was happening in my garden? After discussing the garden problems with Dad and Grandpa, my garden mentors, I learned what I was doing wrong—and boy was it embarrassing. I had been planting in the same soil for years, without adding compost, fertilizers, or any nutrients at all. I'm surprised those poor plants had enough strength to even make leaves!

That lesson taught me how important it is to choose good soil for your garden and to take care of it. Garden soil is full of living creatures—worms, microbes, fungus, and more—and all of these provide nutrients to your plants. Rich, healthy soil is essential for a healthy, vigorous garden. This chapter is dedicated to everything you need to know to give your seeds and plants the best possible start.

All Soil Is Not Created Equal

Did you know that soil and dirt are not the same thing? Dirt may contain sand, silt, clay, or rocks—but it doesn't have any of the organic materials or nutrients that soil does. Soil is a complex mixture of organic matter, water, air, minerals, and living organisms. These materials provide the nutrition plants need to grow, and when growing food, it's important to use fertile, healthy soil.

Healthy soil creates plants that

- Have stronger, better-developed roots
- Are less stressed by differences in soil temperature
- Have better growth overall
- Are more resistant to diseases and insect damage.

STRONGER ROOTS

Strong roots are key for your vegetables, fruits, and herbs. Roots take up air, water, and nutrients from the soil and move them up into the leaves for photosynthesis. Because container plants have a small amount of soil to draw nutrients from, you want to be sure you're providing the best soil to encourage future growth.

Healthy soil is called loam, which means it contains a bit of sand and clay, but mostly decayed vegetable matter and organisms. Loamy soil has tiny pockets for air and water and is full of nutrients. If the soil is primarily clay, the water can't drain, and the roots rot. If the soil contains a lot of sand, the water drains right through, and the plant doesn't have a chance to use it.

Some years in the garden are better than others. When my russet potatoes grew only to the size of golf balls, I learned that depleted soil was the culprit.

The roots of a plant can reach far into the soil—a healthy root system sometimes extends out farther than the plant itself.

STEADY TEMPERATURE

While you wouldn't want to insulate your attic with soil, healthy soil that is well aerated is a natural insulator. When plants are in a large pot, the volume of soil protects the roots from hot afternoon sun and cold nights. This won't make your plants frostproof, but it can protect them from extreme temperature swings.

BETTER GROWTH

All plants grow better in healthy soil because they have access to more nutrients. This is especially important when growing food in containers. Here plants have a finite amount of soil available to them, and you're going to eat the food they produce. In poor-quality soil, container plants may not survive and/or will not produce—just like my failed garden from years ago.

DISEASE AND INSECT RESISTANCE

It makes sense that a healthy plant can survive an attack from insects like aphids or earwigs. A small amount of insect damage won't automatically kill a plant. But did you know that healthy soil can actually help plants fight off some pests and diseases? This is fascinating stuff. Scientists have recently learned that soil microbes can help plants fight off some diseases, which is called "induced systemic resistance." While the research was conducted on large commercial farms, healthy soil full of microbes and other microscopic organisms is essential for home gardeners as well.

Artichokes require a large container, but they make up for it by producing abundantly.

Zucchini, or summer squash, grow quickly and are best harvested when still small.

What's in the Bag?

What's the best soil for your container food garden? Look for a growing medium that's lightweight, well aerated, and contains a good balance of organic and mineral materials.

There are about half a zillion kinds of bagged soils at the garden center, and it can be a bit overwhelming for a new gardener. The different product names are tricky, and the bags don't always explain what's inside. You always want to read the label carefully. You can even mix up your own potting soil with the DIY recipe on page 98.

TYPES OF BAGGED SOIL

Potting soil or potting mix is the best choice for container gardening. Quality potting soil is made of a mixture of materials, usually peat moss or coco coir, perlite or vermiculite, and compost. This combination is light and airy, which allows water and air to move through it easily. It also contains nutrients from the compost and other organic ingredients it may contain. If you look at this ingredient list, you'll see that potting soil doesn't contain any soil at all!

Topsoil is the top layer of soil on the Earth, and a bag of topsoil could contain just about anything. It could be rich and fertile, it could be full of sand, might contain chunks of wood and rocks, or even have a few hitchhiking insects. It's not recommended for container gardening.

Garden soil is heavy and dense, and in a container this can cause soil compaction and root rot. Most bags of garden soil specifically say, "for in-ground use." You also don't want to scoop up soil from your existing in-ground garden because it could contain fungus, microbes, seeds, bugs, or other critters that you don't want in your containers.

Seed starting mix is lightweight and good for temporary use (such as starting seeds indoors), but it doesn't have the nutrients or structure needed for long-term growing.

Planting mix usually contains slow-release fertilizers and is designed for growing shrubs or trees in the ground. These fertilizers are too concentrated for growing food in containers, so don't use planting mix without carefully reading the ingredients.

Moisture-control mix is a soil blend that contains small polymer crystals that absorb lots of water (sort of like the stuff in disposable diapers). These crystals retain the water and don't release it properly to the plant, so skip the moisture-control mix in your container garden.

All soils are not created equal. Look for container gardening soil or potting soil to give your plants the best start. Add compost if it's not already in the mix.

Most commercial potting soils contain a fertilizer that feeds plants through the first few weeks of their lives.

Soil or amendment?

Soils and amendments are two different things. Soil is a mixture of organic matter, water, air, minerals, and living organisms. An amendment is something you add to the soil to improve one or more of its physical or chemical properties. Compost, chicken manure, and vermiculite are examples of soil amendments. Please do not use a bag of soil amendment instead of soil! You can learn more about different types of soil amendments in Chapter 7.

Reading the Soil Bag

If you can't find a potting soil mixture that's specifically labeled for containers, or if you're buying potting soil in bulk, here's what to look for:

- The ingredients should include peat moss or coco coir, perlite or vermiculite, and compost or worm castings. There shouldn't be large pieces of bark, twigs, or leaves in it.

- Squeeze a bit of damp soil in your hand. It should hold together briefly and come apart easily. This is called loam soil. If it clumps like a ball of clay, it's too dense for gardening. If you squeeze it and it falls apart, it's too sandy.

- You want a soil mixture that's porous, lightweight, and smells nice—like the forest floor.

- The soil shouldn't have any bugs emerging from it or seeds sprouting in it.

Ideal container planting soil holds together briefly when squeezed and comes apart easily. Soil that clumps has too much clay and soil that falls apart has too much sand.

Peat Moss vs. Coco Coir

Believe it or not, even the gardening world has its controversies. One of the big discussions you might hear about is the use of peat moss in gardens.

PEAT MOSS

Peat, sometimes called peat moss or sphagnum peat moss, is a soil amendment. It's excellent at retaining water and is made from partially decomposed plants. Sphagnum peat moss is peat that's primarily made from (you guessed it) sphagnum moss.

Peat is created in specific types of wetlands with names you'll recognize—like fen, bog, marsh, or moor. In this waterlogged, acidic medium, dead organisms and plants don't completely decompose. Over centuries, these remains are compacted to form peat.

It's chock-full of organic material and is important for ecosystems and soil development in the areas where it's created. Most peat deposits are in cold climates, like Canada, Russia, Finland, Ireland, Scotland, Germany, and Sweden. It forms extremely slowly—at the rate of about an inch (3 cm) every 15–25 years. While some people say that it can be sustainably harvested, its slow regrowth rate contradicts that statement.

Peat is a fantastic addition to potting soil. It lightens the mix, allows air to enter, holds moisture without being soggy, and generally improves the structure. Sounds amazing, right? But peat takes centuries to form and is a nonrenewable resource. So, what's a gardener to do?

COCO COIR

Thankfully, there is a substitute for peat that works just as well without damaging the environment. It's called coco coir (pronounced *core*). Coco coir is ground coconut-husk fiber, and it's a by-product of coconut processing. Because coconut trees can produce up to 50 coconuts a year, this is a renewable resource that's now being kept out of landfills.

During coconut processing, the coconut meat is separated from the fibrous husks. The husks used to be thrown away, but now they're washed, shredded, and sterilized to become coco coir. Then the coir is compressed into bricks or bales for retail or industrial use. Coco coir goes by a variety of names and can have different textures, so look for coco coir pith or cocopeat when shopping.

Coco coir retains moisture and is loose enough to also provide good drainage and aeration. This helps plants grow healthy roots. Coir takes more than 20 years to decompose.

There are two downsides to coco coir, though. It doesn't contain nutrients, so it needs to be mixed with compost, worm castings, etc. before planting in it. Low-quality coir may contain a lot of salt, so look for a well-known brand that's marked "low salt content" or "washed to remove salts."

There are now several commercial brands of potting mix that are made with coir, rather than with peat moss. You used to have to make your own soil mix if you wanted to use coir, but now there are preblended brands available for purchase.

Make Potting Soil

Making your own potting soil/potting mix is a fantastic and simple DIY project—and if you're filling several containers, it's the most economical choice. Wait, you might be saying, "Who even thinks of making their own soil?!" Well, I have a long history of making things instead of buying them, and I started my website to share these kinds of DIY recipes and gardening tips. When you visit my website, you'll be one of the millions of readers around the world who now says, "Make it, don't buy it!"

Here are just a few of the reasons why I recommend that you make your own potting mix:

- **Save money.** Homemade potting soil works great and is half the price of the bagged kind. If you make your own compost, it's even cheaper.

- **Save time.** Once you have a batch of soil mixed up, you can use it anytime without making an extra trip to the garden center. (If you're like me, staying away from the garden center will also save you money!)

- **Control the ingredients.** You can make your soil with organic ingredients, conventional ingredients, or a combination. You'll know that there aren't any water-retaining chemicals or incompatible fertilizers in your soil.

- **Control the quality.** Many bagged soil mixes contain filler material that can rob nutrients from the soil or will compact and become moisture resistant over time.

MIX YOUR OWN POTTING SOIL

Assemble your materials:

Coco coir: ground coconut husk fiber, which retains moisture and aerates soil

Compost: decaying plant material that adds nutrients, improves soil structure, adds beneficial microbes and bacteria

Perlite: a specific type of volcanic glass that puffs up when heated; improves soil aeration

Vermiculite: a silicate mineral that expands when heated; retains moisture

Worm castings: earthworm poop; adds lots of nutrients plus beneficial microbes and bacteria

Measuring device: a scoop of any size—I'm using a plastic 4-cup (500 ml) measuring cup

Water: a hose or watering can

Wheelbarrow: or large bucket for mixing

Gardening gloves

Dust or face mask

Shovel: if mixing a large quantity

Instructions:

Because dry perlite and vermiculite can release tiny mineral particles—which you don't want to inhale—always wear a mask over your nose and mouth when making this recipe.

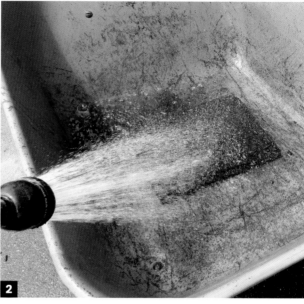

1 Coco coir comes in a compressed brick and must be rehydrated before using. This is ¼ of the brick shown above, and this piece alone will expand into more than 30 cups (7 L) of coco coir when rehydrated.

2 Hydrate the coir by putting it in a wheelbarrow or large bin and drenching it with water. It will expand tremendously as it absorbs the water.

3 The inside of this chunk of coco coir is light brown because it's not hydrated yet. Keep adding water and breaking up the pieces until all the coir is uniformly dark brown and damp. Then it's time to measure and combine the ingredients.

4 In the wheelbarrow or bucket, combine

- 2 scoops coco coir
- 2 scoops compost
- 1 scoop perlite
- ½ scoop vermiculite
- ½ scoop worm castings

5 Mix all the ingredients thoroughly with a shovel or your gloved hands. When everything is thoroughly mixed and moistened, grab a handful and squeeze. It should be a loamy texture—coming together easily and then falling apart. If the soil stays in a solid clump, add half a scoop of coco coir. If it won't hold together, add half a scoop of compost.

Your container soil is ready to use! Store any extra soil covered in a cool, dry place.

Reusing Potting Soil

Should you reuse your potting soil every year? This is a topic that a lot of gardeners feel strongly about. One theory says that if there are diseases in the soil, you'll circumvent them by replacing the soil every year. And over time, the perlite and vermiculite can compact, which leads to dense soil and poor drainage. But, as you can imagine, replacing the soil every year is quite expensive.

If the plants in your container somehow get diseased (unlikely, but it happens, especially with tomato and potato family members growing in the same soil during successive years) then you should absolutely get rid of the soil and start fresh. You'll also need to sterilize the container—instructions for that are in Chapter 3.

Most of the time, it's fine to reuse potting soil. Before planting a new crop in the same soil, be sure to add compost and/or worm castings and mix them in thoroughly. This will add nutrients back into the soil and revitalize it for your new plants.

Soil What-ifs

What if water runs off the top of the soil or directly out of the drain holes without soaking into the soil?
This means the soil has become hydrophobic (resistant to water) and needs to be carefully re-wetted. If you can, soak the entire container in a large bucket of water. The soil will probably float at first, and there will be lots of bubbles as the air in the soil escapes. Pull the container out of the water once the bubbles stop.

If the container is too big to move, water the plant very slowly with a dripping garden hose. This slow trickle of water will absorb into the soil, but it might take an hour or two. You can also poke holes in the soil (away from the plant's roots) with a long stick or chopstick. This will help the water penetrate the soil and reach the roots.

If the soil doesn't absorb water, it may have dried out completely and become hydrophobic. The soil must be carefully rehydrated to save the plant.

What if the soil has shrunk away from the sides of the container, or the plant is sinking into the soil?
Soil compacts, sinks, and shrinks when it's completely dried out. If the soil has become so dry that it resists water, use the preceding suggestions to rehydrate it. If there simply isn't enough soil in the container, you can add more. Gently tip the plant out of the container, add more soil, and replant (see step-by-step instructions in Chapter 1). If you can't remove the plant from the container, sprinkle more soil into the pot and gently mix it into the existing soil.

Ensure your container veggie garden receives plenty of sunlight. Six hours of full sun is the minimum needed for most vegetables.

5

Sun & Location

For years and years, our vegetable garden was in a tiny corner of our backyard next to our pool. The kids and their friends played and splashed next to green beans, tomatoes, pumpkins, and zucchini. We grew quite a bit of food, but there wasn't enough space or sun to grow everything I wanted. The front yard was a wide-open canvas, and it got a lot more sunlight. But was I brave enough to remove the lawn and grow vegetables? That was the real question.

I started out small, growing chard and artichokes in half-barrel planters. I figured if anybody complained, I could move the planters to the backyard—but nobody seemed to mind. My daughter and I planted strawberries and flowers in the front yard and our neighbors would visit with us while we gardened. Some of them even asked about growing vegetables in their yards!

Over the years, we added more plants to our front yard garden. The kids and I planted container blueberries, raspberries, an apricot tree, plus jalapeño peppers and cherry tomatoes. Now both the front garden and back garden are superproductive, and our family enjoys vegetables and fruits from them all year long.

Why do I mention this? Because sometimes the best sunlight for your garden is in an unconventional location. Your apartment balcony might be shaded all day long—but can you garden on the roof? Maybe your yard is the size of a postage stamp. Try growing herbs and strawberries vertically, on the fence. You have lots of options, even if you have to think creatively. And since you're growing in containers, you can move plants around and try different locations to see what works best.

Let's dive into the details so you can find the best, sunniest spot for your garden.

How Much Sun?

Plant tags, seed packets, and gardening books use specific terms to express how much sunlight a plant needs to thrive. It's important to know what these terms mean, so you can choose the right plants for the amount of sun your garden gets throughout the day.

Full Sun: Plants that need full sun require at least 6 hours of direct sunlight each day, without any shade. Gardeners in northern climates will have better results if the plants receive 8 hours of direct sunlight each day. More sun won't hurt these plants—they're suited to hot, sunny climates. If you grow full-sun plants in an area that gets fewer than 6 hours of direct sun per day, they won't automatically die—they'll just be smaller and produce less than they would in optimal conditions. Tomatoes, zucchini, and peppers are a few of the many vegetables that need full sun.

Partial Shade: These plants need from 3–6 hours of direct sunlight each day. Most of the time, this means morning sun and afternoon shade. The sun is hottest in the afternoon, so a bit of shade during that time protects these plants. They'll also do well in dappled sun, which is when the sunlight is filtered through trees or a sunshade. Some examples of partial shade vegetables are cucumbers, beans, and peas.

Full Shade: Plants that thrive in full shade need fewer than 3 hours of direct sunlight, usually in the morning. These tend to be delicate plants, and if they are accidentally planted in full sun they'll die. There aren't many vegetables that grow in full shade, but lettuce and spinach will grow in conditions pretty close to full shade. Note: zero hours of direct sunlight is called dense shade, and there are very few plants that will grow in those conditions.

Sun Combinations: Sometimes a plant tag will use a combination of these terms, like "Full sun to partial shade." This gives you more flexibility in growing, because it means the plant is adaptable to a wider range of conditions.

MEASURING SUNLIGHT

As mentioned, most vegetables and fruits need 6–8 hours of sun per day to thrive. The amount of light your yard gets will change throughout the day, as shadows from trees and buildings pass over your garden. Most vegetables will grow and produce just fine with a bit of morning or afternoon shade.

Remember that the sunlight will change from spring to summer, and some areas might get more or less sun over time. The good thing about container gardens is you can move the pots as needed to adapt to the sunlight your garden receives.

Figuring out where the light falls throughout the day is called *sun mapping*, and there are several ways to do it. The following methods are in order from least precise to most precise.

A bit of creative thinking will help you garden wherever you are. This herb garden is happily growing on the backyard fence.

Combine plants with similar sunlight needs in the same container. These stunning red lettuces, and the herbs behind them, all need partial shade to thrive.

Direction

Which direction does your patio face, or what side of the house is your garden on? This is a simple way to figure out what parts of your yard will be the sunniest throughout the day. It doesn't take into account things like shade from buildings, trees, and the like—but if you're moving to a new city or neighborhood, or are choosing which side of an apartment building to rent, this will give you a head start.

- **North:** Shady during the day, with evening sun in summer and fall.

- **South:** The best location! Warm and sunny all day, with a longer growing season.

- **East:** Morning sun and shade for the rest of the day.

- **West:** Shade in the morning, hot and sunny the rest of the day.

Google Earth

Use Google Earth to get an idea of where the sunny spots are in your yard. Keep in mind that this is a snapshot of one moment in time, so it won't show how the sunlight changes throughout the day. If you combine the picture from Google Earth with the direction information above, you can get an idea of how much sunlight you'll be working with in the garden.

As the name implies, snow peas prefer the cold weather and the gentle sunlight of early spring. Other vegetables are better suited for hot, direct summer sun.

Because of the fence and the direction the house faces, this backyard is shaded even though it doesn't have any trees.

Observation

Start early in the morning, right after sunrise. Check your garden area every 2 hours, observing which parts of your yard are sunny, which are shady, and which have dappled sun. You may want to take notes or make a sketch on graph paper so you don't forget. Keep checking and recording until sunset.

Photo Mapping

Photo mapping is a bit time consuming, but it gives the most accurate results. Place your camera on a tripod and set it somewhere that allows a good view of your potential garden area. You want to take all the photos from the same spot and at the same angle. Higher is better, so you get as much of the area in the picture as possible. Take a photo every hour at roughly the same time (for example, at 6:15 am, 7:15 am, and so on throughout the day).

Once you have an entire day's worth of pictures, it's time to analyze where the sun is. You can examine the photos or stack them with photo-editing software to see which parts of the yard stay sunny the longest.

There are garden gizmos called "light meters" that, once set into the soil, will tell you how much sunlight an area has at that moment. I suggest that instead of buying one of these expensive devices, you use one of the free methods listed above. Save your money for buying plants!

Wind

It's true that you can't stop the wind from blowing—but you can plan for it and mitigate its effects on your garden. Strong winds can dry out soil, damage leaves, and knock down plants. Wind also increases cold damage, so your plants could suffer from wind chill even though temperatures are mild.

High winds can knock down tall and narrow containers, especially if they're top-heavy. Trees, tomatoes, and other tall, bushy plants can catch the wind and fall over. This can damage the harvest or cause the stem to snap, killing the plant completely.

Prolonged winds can sometimes cause problems in the garden too. Flowers can dry out and become less attractive to pollinators, which leads to reduced pollination and therefore less fruit. Leaves get damaged or torn, causing stress to the plant overall.

Balcony and rooftop gardens are especially prone to damage because they are continuously exposed to wind. Tall buildings can channel and concentrate wind, like the way a hose nozzle turns a trickle of water into a powerful spray.

After reading this, you might be panicking a little, but don't worry! If you're gardening in windy conditions, there are lots of ways to protect your plants. Some of these ideas are permanent and some are temporary, which makes them great for renters.

PREVENTING WIND DAMAGE

Plants that are stressed or damaged by wind will produce a smaller harvest, if they produce at all. It's better to protect plants from wind damage than try and heal them after the fact. There are several ways to keep excess wind from damaging your container plants.

Tomatoes, strawberries, lettuce, and other plants that grow in hanging baskets need extra protection on windy days.

The windbreak on this balcony railing protects the containers on the patio from strong winds.

LEFT: Strawberries, violas, and nasturtium add a pop of delicious color to the front yard garden.

After a bit of sun mapping, you may need to think creatively to get your plants the sun they need.

Structural Methods

To slow the wind down with a natural windbreak, arrange your plants so the tall ones shelter the shorter ones. This might cause the shorter plants to be shaded, so keep an eye on the sun to be sure they're getting enough light.

If you're gardening on a balcony, attach permeable fabric to the balcony railings. You can buy special windbreak netting or use weed barrier cloth with small holes cut in it. Be sure to securely attach the windbreak to the railing, so the fabric won't flap around in the wind and damage your plants.

Choose nonporous containers, like metal, glazed ceramic, or plastic. Constant wind is less likely to dry out the soil in these types of planters.

Use larger containers, especially if you're growing in fabric or plastic. If the soil in a small plastic pot dries out, it's likely to blow over or even blow away. This can damage or kill your plant.

Place planters against the wall of a building or in a corner of the balcony. If the shape of the container allows it, carefully secure the planter to the balcony railing with brackets (or use rope in a pinch).

Plant a vertical container garden against a wall or another protected surface.

This rooftop garden is exposed to constant wind. Pole beans are supported with tripod structures that are more stable than a flat trellis.

Plant-Specific Ideas

- Stake or cage tomatoes, and plant them in a heavy pot with a wide base. This adds stability and makes the container less likely to tip over.

- Use a tripod structure for cucumbers and pole beans instead of a traditional flat trellis, which turns into a sail when the plants fully cover it.

- Secure plants that don't normally need to be staked, like peppers and okra.

- Cover smaller plants or seedlings with a glass or plastic covering called a cloche.

- If possible, bring plants inside during extreme winds.

Low-growing plants like lettuces and herbs can withstand a windy location better than taller plants, which are likely to tip over.

If you're in a windy spot and can't install a windbreak, then choose low-growing edible plants such as

- Bush beans
- Chard
- Chives
- Garlic
- Kale
- Lettuce
- Oregano
- Parsley
- Potatoes
- Radish
- Rosemary
- Sage
- Thyme

Don't build a solid fence around your garden to protect it from wind. The wind will fly over the top and come crashing down, without slowing, and will damage your plants.

Microclimates

A microclimate is a specific area that has a different climate than the area that surrounds it. The difference in climate can be caused by sunlight, rain, wind, and other factors. In nature, microclimates occur everywhere. For example, a sunny hillside might support completely different plant life than the shady valley below.

Within your container vegetable garden, there are natural microclimates as well. They can be caused by the slope of the land, sun exposure, and structures like fences or patios. Figuring out these microclimates—and even creating some of your own—can help improve your garden.

IDENTIFYING MICROCLIMATES

Before we dive into creating microclimates in your garden, let's work with what's already there. Here are some factors to consider when determining what microclimates already exist where you live:

Taking advantage of microclimates can really enhance the production of your container garden. Warm weather–loving crops situated against a dark wall that retains heat are one example.

East, West, North, and South

Directions matter a lot when it comes to microclimates. Think about how the sunlight hits your space. Is it coming mostly from the east or north? From these directions, sunlight is less direct and produces a cool, moist environment. If the sunlight is coming from the west or south, chances are your garden will be warm and dry. You can place your containers in different areas to maximize or minimize their sun exposure.

Elevation

The higher parts of your property will tend to be warmer and drier, while low-lying areas will be cooler and retain more moisture. For example, a rooftop garden will be exposed to much more wind and direct sunlight than a balcony garden. The same is true of a backyard garden—strawberries or herbs that are planted in hanging baskets or vertically on a fence will have more wind and sun exposure than those growing on the ground.

Surrounding Structures

Structures can include walls, fences, the sides of buildings, patios, driveways, sidewalks, decks, and so on. These structures can impact microclimates in a few ways. Structures can cool your garden by shading it from the sun, or they can warm your garden by reflecting or absorbing the heat from the sun.

Patios, sidewalks, and driveways absorb heat during the day and release it during the night. Combined with the direction they face, these structures can completely change the microclimates. For instance, a southwest-facing wall next to a patio is going to reflect and hold a lot of heat. The growing conditions there would be hot and dry. A northern-facing wall would have the opposite effect by blocking the most direct sunlight.

Fences, walls, and buildings also protect plants from the wind, which can be helpful year-round. Too much wind can damage plants any time. During the summer, hot winds can parch plants, while in the winter, the wind can cause plants to get too cold.

Trees and Shrubs

Larger trees and shrubs can act like structures in your garden, shielding plants from the hot summer sun or protecting them from the wind. Trees and shrubs also affect the temperature of your garden. For example, a yard full of trees and mature landscaping is a lot cooler than an open, grassy field. Keep this in mind when identifying microclimates.

MICROCLIMATES FOR SPECIFIC VEGETABLES

As you might guess, different vegetables are going to thrive in different microclimates. Once you've identified some obvious microclimates in your space, you can choose to grow plants that will thrive in that spot. Here's a quick rundown on some of the most popular vegetables and what type of microclimate they need:

Peppers and Tomatoes: Peppers and tomatoes need heat and sun. They'll thrive on southern slopes or planted near walls that face south. Slopes and walls will also prevent issues with breakage caused by heavy winds. These plants do especially well near driveways, patios, and sidewalks since these structures retain heat and protect plants from frost damage in the late planting season.

Lettuce and Leafy Greens: These cool-weather crops do well in low-lying areas, on northern slopes, and near shady trees. They'll also thrive in the shade of buildings and walls with morning sunlight. Trees, shrubs, and walls will also provide protection from wind, which can damage these tender, leafy plants.

Peas and Beans: These plants need lots of sun and moisture, so low-lying areas that receive full sun are perfect for all types of peas and beans.

Root Vegetables: Root vegetables like carrots, potatoes, and beets need partial shade. They can handle east-facing slopes better than other plants and can tolerate more wind because they grow underground.

This large planter box is in a challenging microclimate. The buildings' surfaces reflect heat, and the plants must endure a lot of wind. The tomatoes, eggplant, and peppers in this container were chosen because they can survive in these conditions.

Tomatoes need warm soil and full sun, so this microclimate along the south side of the house is the best location for them.

Root vegetables tolerate more wind than some other veggies.

HOW TO CREATE SPECIFIC MICROCLIMATES

Sometimes you might not have just the right climate in your space for the plants you want to grow. Good news! You can augment or create microclimates to improve your container garden.

Warming up a microclimate is a great way to extend the growing season during the cooler months. Cooling down a microclimate can help you keep your container garden going even during the hottest weeks of summer. Here are some ways you can create a warmer or cooler microclimate for your veggie pots:

Creating a Warmer Microclimate

- Place containers near a south-facing wall or fence.

- Set containers on concrete or blacktop instead of on soil.

- Since cold air tends to sink, containers have an automatic advantage over in-ground gardening. For maximum warming effect, raise containers on a table or bench.

- Without blocking southern or western light, you can plant or build wind barriers to protect plants from cold winds.

- Fill large jugs with water and place them near plants. These will absorb heat during the day and release it during the night.

Creating a Cooler Microclimate

- Creating shade is the best way to create a cool microclimate. You can use structures and large plants to block the southern and western light to drastically reduce the temperature of that part of your container garden.

- Fencing, lattice, and trellises can all be used to add shade for your plants.

- Shade cloth can also be used to create a shadier garden, particularly if you use it to block the southern or western sun during midday and late afternoon.

- Water your containers regularly, preferably in the early morning, to keep the soil cool.

- Mulch (see Chapter 7) is also a great way to keep the soil cool and moist even during the hot, dry months of summer.

The most important plant-care task for container gardens is watering. Learn how to do it properly and you'll reap big rewards.

6

Watering

Just like the years have flown by in the garden, they've flown by for our family too. The kids have grown up and now spend their weekends writing essays and studying for tests instead of helping me in the garden. They still enjoy eating all the fruits and vegetables I grow, though!

We recently took a road trip through California's Central Valley to visit prospective colleges in Southern California. This part of the state is absolutely chock-full of farms and orchards, and produces more than half of the fruits, vegetables, and nuts grown in the United States. Many of these farms are planted within feet of the freeway in amazingly rich, fertile soil. As the miles passed, we enjoyed looking at all the crops and figuring out what was growing on these vast acres of farmland.

It happened to be really windy during our trip, and one of the farms was watering with giant overhead sprinklers. They were similar to pop-up lawn sprinklers but were raised on poles more than 8 feet (2.4 m) high. The wind was blowing so hard that more water seemed to be spraying on the freeway than on the plants! It was an unusually windy day, but this method didn't seem like the most water-wise choice for irrigation.

Why do I mention this? We all know that container vegetables need water, but the way that you water them matters. Let's talk about smart watering that takes care of your plants and doesn't waste this precious resource.

WHEN TO WATER

While you might water your lawn on a strict schedule, watering your container garden requires a little more finesse. As much as I would like to think about watering only three times a week, that's not realistic for potted plants. There are many variables that affect your garden's watering needs:

- **Type and age of plants** Newly planted seeds and seedlings need to be gently watered once or twice a day; mature plants may need to be watered only every few days.

- **Container material, size, and porosity** Plants in small containers made of porous material need to be watered more frequently than plants in a large, nonporous container.

- **Soil quality** The best container soil mix holds water as well as air, so plants can absorb nutrients and bring them up to the leaves for photosynthesis.

- **Sun and wind exposure** Plants in full sun and windy conditions (like rooftop gardens) need to be watered daily.

- **Weather, rain, and humidity** Areas that get rain during the growing season may only need to be watered occasionally to supplement rainfall.

CHECK THE SOIL

You don't need a fancy moisture meter or other garden gizmo to see if your plants need water—just use your finger or a wooden chopstick. Stick your finger or chopstick at least 2 inches (5 cm) into the soil—if the soil feels damp or sticks to your finger or the chopstick, there's enough moisture. If they come up dry with no soil sticking to them, it's time to water.

Here in California, we don't get summertime rain. I check my containers every day, and since they're heavily mulched (see Chapter 7 for information about using mulch) they need to be watered only every few days.

An easy way to see if a container needs water is by inserting a clean chopstick a few inches into the soil. If soil sticks to the chopstick, then the soil is damp and doesn't need to be watered.

Citrus trees, like this dwarf lemon, need large containers and deep watering for optimal growth.

TIME OF DAY

What's the best time of day to water your plants? This is a simple answer—when the plants need it. While morning is the ideal time to water, please don't look at your wilting peas and say, "Sorry, guys, it's 2 pm and the book says I can't water you until 6 am tomorrow!"

- Water in the morning if you can. This allows any excess water to evaporate off leaves, which helps prevent fungus and mildew.

- If you water in the evening, be careful to only wet the soil—not the leaves of the plants. Cold and wet leaves are susceptible to mildew, fungus, and leaf diseases.

- Afternoon heat makes it tough for plants to get all the water they need, but if the soil is dry and the plants need water, don't wait.

Morning is the best time to water, but if you see wilted leaves, water right away.

What kind of water?

Does your container vegetable garden need special water? You may see suggestions to use distilled water, bottled water, or rainwater/melted snow in your container garden. This is unnecessary, impractical, and expensive. Most of the time, water from the hose or tap is just fine for your plants.

How to Water

I've seen a lot of folks spray the hose around for 3 or 4 minutes and declare that their watering chores are done. This gets the leaves wet but doesn't do much for the soil where the water is needed. Plants need strong roots, and this means watering deeply so the roots grow down. Light watering causes shallow root growth, which equals weak plants.

LOW AND SLOW

When watering your containers, think low and slow. Put your hose or watering device low to the soil, and let the water run slowly into the container.

Why water the soil and not the leaves? Plants absorb very little water through their leaves—water must go into the soil to be used. Putting the water at the soil level allows it to run through the entire soil mass, which encourages roots to grow down. Plants with deep roots are better equipped to withstand drought, wind, and other stressful conditions.

Slow watering allows time for the water to reach the soil throughout the container. Have you ever seen soil wash away during a heavy rain? That's what can happen if water is quickly blasted from a hose sprayer. When watering seeds or seedlings, it's very important to water slowly and gently. The force of water from the hose can wash the seeds right out of the container!

After a low-and-slow watering session, you should see water seeping out of the drainage holes. This means you've wet the entire soil mass, which is good for the plant and also helps with soil leaching. Soil leaching gives soil a thorough rinse, which helps wash away damaging buildup from fertilizer salts.

If your containers have saucers or drip trays, come back and empty them about 30 minutes after watering. Leaving water in the saucer deprives your plant roots of oxygen, which can cause root rot. The water in the saucer also contains the salts that have leached out of the soil, which you don't want the plants to reabsorb.

Large containers need more water than small containers, even if the plant inside is still small.

Can I water by filling up the saucer?

Yes, you can water your plants occasionally by filling up the saucer and letting them absorb the water from the bottom as needed. This is called bottom watering, and it is how many houseplants are watered. For outdoor plants, though, it's best to water from the top (most of the time) to ensure that the soil is being leached of salts.

RIGHT: Water the soil, not the leaves. This allows the roots to absorb the water and helps prevent mildew from forming on the leaves. These popcorn plants are less likely to develop rust and other fungal diseases.

Watering Methods/ Equipment

If you have a container garden in the front yard and the backyard like I do, set up a watering station in both areas. I have long, lightweight garden hoses with a rain wand in both areas. That way I won't put off watering because I don't have the tools I need! Here are the best ways to water your container plants.

Hose with spray nozzle

This is my favorite way to water container plants. Using the hose without a nozzle can wash soil right out of the pot, so use a spray nozzle or rain wand on the "shower" or "rain" setting. Remember to water the soil and not the leaves. This method takes only a few minutes, and you can check on the health of your plants while you're watering. If you see that a plant has a few aphids on it, for example, you can simply wash the aphids off before they do any damage.

Watering can

Depending on the size of your garden, a watering can might be efficient or it might be tiring. In a small patio or porch, a watering can is fine. If you're taking the stairs to a rooftop garden or are running between the front yard and backyard, another method will be better. I use a large, metal watering can with a top and side handle and a rosette, or sprinkler-head, spout. This breaks up the force of the water, unlike free-flowing spouts which can wash away soil.

Automatic sprinkler

Sprinklers make watering easy, but sometimes this system can cause problems. If the sprinklers spray water on the plants from overhead, the plants will be susceptible to fungus or mildew. Sprinklers that have attachments for each container are an improvement over a lawn sprinkler that sprays over the whole yard. If you're using attachments for each container, ensure the spray stays inside the container and that the sprinkler runs long enough to wet the entire soil mass.

RIGHT: A watering can with a rosette spout is easier on plants than a free-flow spout, which has a strong stream that can wash away soil.

Drip irrigation is an extremely efficient way to water a container garden, but it does require money and time to set up. These bean plants growing in fabric pots have a drip irrigation set up to regularly water them.

Drip lines

Drip lines can be made from garden hoses with tiny holes that drip water into the soil, or they can be individual sprinkler lines with an attachment that drips water into the container. While these can be complicated to set up, they always water low and slow. There are a few drawbacks, though. Because the water drips out of a tiny hole, if you run it for a short period of time, it only wets the soil in the immediate area. You have to make sure you leave it on long enough for the water to wick through the entire pot and fully water all of the soil. If the drip attachment clogs, or if the system doesn't run long enough, your plants won't get enough water.

Summer rain

Some climates get rain in the summertime, but you shouldn't rely on this as the only way to water your container garden. Lush foliage can also sometimes block rain from reaching the soil. It's best to check your containers a day or two after it rains to see if they need to be watered again.

Water helps protect plants from temperature swings

Many climates have major temperature changes from day to night—very hot during the day and cold at night, for example. Careful watering and planting in a large container will help your soil keep a more even temperature range throughout the day. Add extra compost to the soil and top it with mulch to keep water from evaporating. This will help keep your plants insulated and protect them from the stress of extreme temperature changes.

Vacation Watering

Many gardeners take vacations during the growing season or need to travel for work and will be away from home. Leaving your precious container garden can be nerve wracking, and it can be hard to relax and enjoy your vacation if you're imagining your plants languishing in the heat!

With a little bit of planning, your container garden will survive your absence just fine. You may even come back to find a new crop that's ready to harvest. There are several ways to keep your container plantings alive while you're gone, even if there isn't anyone around to water them.

WATERING WHILE AWAY METHODS

- If you're hiring a house sitter or pet sitter, they can water for you. Be sure to give them clear instructions and add it to their checklist so they don't forget.

- Water thoroughly before you leave and add mulch to your planters to retain moisture in the soil. See page 145 for details on the best mulches for your container garden.

- Move your plants to a shady spot. A few days in the shade won't hurt them, and they won't need as much water as usual since they're in the shade. If you have containers that you can't move, put a patio umbrella over them or rig up a shade cloth.

- Use a watering stake, which is a large glass or plastic sphere with a narrow stem. Fill it with water, push the stem deep into the soil, and the water drips out slowly over time. I use a homemade version, which is a plastic water bottle with holes punched in the lid.

Finding a way to water container plants while you're away on vacation requires a bit of creativity.

- Make a wicking system. Fill a large can or bucket with water and place it on a box or shelf above the planter. Cut a long piece of cotton string or butcher's twine that reaches from the bottom of the can, all the way up and into the soil of the container. Tie a washer or small fishing weight on one end of the string and put that end in the can full of water. Bury the other end a few inches deep into the container, and water will wick from the can into the container as needed.

- Set up a sprinkler drip system on a timer. This is a big project to tackle right before a trip, but it can be done.

Rain Barrels

Rain barrels are large containers that are connected to your roof downspouts. They collect rain from your roof, which prevents rainwater from eroding the soil in your yard and spilling into the storm drain. Rain barrels are great for conserving water and saving money on your water bill!

If they're legal in your area (in some places they are not), the water utility may have suggestions or discounts for you. They require a connector kit to run the water into the barrel, and a mesh cover to prevent mosquitos from laying eggs in the water. The barrel has a spigot at the bottom that can be used to connect a hose or fill up watering cans. It should be fully closed to keep children and animals from accidentally falling into it.

Rain barrel water is safe to use on the lawn or flower beds and containers, but it shouldn't be used on edible plants. Roofing materials can leach chemicals into the water, and you just don't know what other kinds of contaminants are on your roof. Think about the birds, squirrels, rats, and other critters that run across the roof every day and where their little feet have been (ick). Bacteria like *E. coli* and parasites from animal poop will be washed into the rain barrel from the roof, so please don't use this water in your vegetable garden.

Rain barrels are great for conserving water, but this water should be used on lawns and shrubs, not edible plants.

Water Woes

What if water runs off the top of the soil and doesn't soak in?

This means the soil has become hydrophobic (resistant to water) and needs to be carefully re-wetted. If you can, soak the entire container in a large bucket of water. The soil will probably float at first, and there will be lots of bubbles as the air in the soil escapes. Pull the container out of the water once the bubbles stop.

If the container is too big to move, water the plant very slowly with a dripping garden hose. This slow trickle of water will absorb into the soil, but it might take an hour or two. You can also poke holes in the soil (away from the plant's roots) with a long stick or chopstick. This will help the water penetrate the soil and reach the roots.

What if water isn't coming out of the drain holes?

If you're giving the plant enough water but nothing's coming out the bottom, the drain holes are probably clogged with roots or a clump of soil. Carefully tip the container on its side. If roots are growing out of the drain holes, the container is too small and the plant needs to be replanted in a larger pot. If you don't see any roots, use a pencil or chopstick to poke up through the drain holes and loosen the soil.

Signs of underwatering:

- Soil is dry and pulls away from the edges of the container
- Leaf tips turn brown
- Older leaves turn yellow or brown and fall off
- Leaves droop and don't recover by morning
- Stems or branches die back
- Papery or thin leaves

Signs of overwatering:

- Water consistently comes out of the drain holes
- Soil is constantly damp
- Leaves turn light green or yellow
- Mushrooms are growing in container
- Roots are black/brown and mushy
- Mold is on the soil

Attracting Pollinators

Pollinating insects and birds play an important role in creating a healthy, bountiful vegetable garden. With the right plants and a few simple tips, you can easily attract beneficial pollinators to your container garden. Any animal that carries pollen from plant to plant is considered a pollinator. By picking up and distributing pollen, these animals help fertilize plants so they can produce seeds or fruit.

The most common pollinators include bees, hummingbirds, butterflies, moths, and some songbirds. These garden friends visit flowers to drink nectar and happen to pick up a little pollen along the way. When they visit the next flower, some of the pollen is left behind. Technically, other pollinators can include bats, wasps, beetles, spiders, and some small mammals. But we're just going to stick to the most common (and most efficient!) pollinators here.

Bees are one of the many pollinators in your garden along with hummingbirds, butterflies, and other insects.

BENEFITS OF POLLINATORS

So, why should you be thinking about how to attract more pollinators to your container garden? There are a few very good reasons you want more pollinators around, but the most important one for a vegetable garden (container or otherwise) is a better harvest.

No matter what you're planting, good pollination will increase the yields from your garden. Some plants like cucumbers, pumpkins, squashes, and watermelon require pollination to produce healthy fruit. Other plants can produce fruit through self-pollination (like tomatoes, peppers, and green beans), but even these will produce better yields when cross-pollinated from visits by pollinators. No matter what vegetables you plant, you'll get more out of your garden when there are plenty of pollinators around.

Other benefits include

- **Natural pest management.** Some pollinators (certain wasps and beetles, for example) are natural predators of garden pests like aphids. Attracting these pollinators is a natural way to control pests in your container veggie garden.

- **It's good for the local ecosystem.** Pollinating species have had it rough. Between urban development and toxic pesticides, many pollinator populations have decreased in recent years. By providing food and shelter for pollinators, you're actually benefiting the entire local ecosystem in addition to your container veggies.

RIGHT: This chubby bumblebee is quite pleased to pollinate this cucumber flower. Encourage them by having lots of flowering plants in your container garden.

CHOOSING PLANTS FOR POLLINATORS

How do you know which plants to choose to attract pollinators? Pollinators like colorful flowers that produce lots of nectar, and these additional tips will help you choose the best ones to include in your container garden in combination with your edible plants.

- **Go native.** Choose at least some plants that are native to your region. Local birds and insects are most likely to visit plants that are native to their habitat.

- **Aim for blooms all spring and summer.** You'll need pollinators all season long, so choose a variety of plants that will bloom at successive times (early spring, late spring, early summer, etc.). This will keep your garden active for more of the growing season.

- **Add a variety of color and shapes.** Bees, butterflies, hummingbirds, and songbirds are all drawn to different colors based on their vision. Try to have some yellows, reds, oranges, purples, and blues in your garden. Also, aim for a variety of flower shapes too. Butterflies like clusters of flat-shaped flowers, while hummingbirds are drawn to trumpet-shaped flowers. If you're planting in a small space, focus on flowers that attract multiple species like heliotrope, sunflowers, aster, or lavender.

- **Don't forget scents.** Pollinators like good-smelling plants too! Choose fragrant flowers and herbs to plant around your garden. Basil, lavender, and sage are herbs that are known to attract pollinators.

Pollination partners

Have you ever heard that kittens should be adopted in pairs? This is recommended so they can play together, grow up together, and generally live their best life. You might be thinking, "What the heck does this have to do with growing food?" Well, many fruit trees and bushes need to be planted in pairs so they will thrive, be well-pollinated, and set fruit. They simply won't produce fruit without being pollinated!

Thankfully, choosing compatible pollination partners is considerably easier than adopting kittens. Keep this information in mind, and don't be nervous to ask for help at your local plant nursery:

- Each species can pollinate only others of its kind (apples with apples, blueberries with blueberries, etc.). However, they must be different varieties of the same species, like a Granny Smith apple and a Fuji apple.

- Choose plants that bloom at the same time, so pollinators can do their work. The grower or plant nursery staff can help you with this.

- Place their containers as close together as possible, to a maximum of 100 feet (30 m) apart.

- If you absolutely can't fit two fruit trees in your garden, choose a self-fertile (self-pollinating) tree (which doesn't need a pollination partner) or a combination tree, which has different varieties of the same species grafted onto the main trunk.

MORE WAYS TO ATTRACT POLLINATORS

Attracting pollinators isn't just about which flowers are in your containers. You want to create an environment that attracts and shelters pollinating species, so they'll visit and stick around. Luckily, this isn't hard to do. Try the following ideas to make your garden a haven for pollinators:

Add a Bird Bath: Some songbirds are pollinators, and they also happen to love a good bath. Place a bird bath in a shady, level spot near your container vegetable garden. Look for a spot with tree branches nearby (birds love to preen their feathers after they've had a soak).

Make sure the water is no more than 2 inches (5 cm) deep. You can place a couple of river rocks in the bath so birds can sit and drink without getting wet too. Check on your bird bath from time to time to make sure it is clean and clear of debris.

Create a Bee and Butterfly Bath: Bees and butterflies can use a bath too! They will come by often for a drink, especially during dry months. Bird baths are too big and too deep for these insects—they need a small, very shallow bath lined with rocks to perch on safely while they get a drink. Keep the bath in a quiet, shady spot near your container garden.

Stick to Natural Pest Control: Harsh chemical pesticides can be toxic to natural pollinators, so this is just another good reason to stick to all-natural pest control. And, as mentioned previously, certain pollinators are natural predators of garden pests, so you get an added benefit when you create a healthy, safe environment for them.

Provide Shelter for Pollinators: Birds, bees, and butterflies alike will appreciate a safe place to shelter that's not out in the open. Flowering shrubs like rhododendrons can pull double duty as a shelter in which pollinators can hide and rest. Some bees like to shelter in sandy soil, rock piles, or dead wood as well.

Birdbaths don't need to be fancy, just clean and full of water.

Bee baths are a fun way to draw more pollinators to your container garden.

Container gardens require fertilization
throughout the season to perform their best.

7

Fertilizing & Soil Amendments

Because container plants have a limited amount of soil to pull nutrients from, fertilizers and soil amendments are essential to ensure you have a good harvest. Using the right fertilizers and amendments makes a big difference in the health of your garden, and you can use natural, synthetic, or a combination of both—the plants don't care. Fertilizers help plants directly by improving the supply of available nutrients in the soil. Amendments help plants grow indirectly by improving the soil.

CHOOSING A FERTILIZER

Trying to pick the right fertilizer can be overwhelming. It's like looking at all the vitamins available at the pharmacy and trying to figure out which one is right for you. Just like there are different human vitamins for various ages and needs, there are many types of fertilizers for different needs in the garden.

Let's look at some of the fertilizer options you'll find for your container garden.

NATURAL VS. SYNTHETIC

Natural fertilizers (including soil amendments like manures and compost) are made from products that occur in nature—like seaweed, bone meal, manure, and various mined minerals, among others. These fertilizers are minimally processed, and they provide nutrients in a form that is slowly released. Many help build soil health over time.

Synthetic fertilizers are made from chemicals and provide a quick "boost" to a plant. They are designed to dissolve—not stay in the soil—so they don't improve the soil over time. However, their nutrients work quickly to support a plant's needs.

Natural fertilizers are like eating healthy food. They keep the soil in optimal condition for the long term. Synthetic fertilizers are like vitamins that help during a time of stress or nutrient deficiency. Both of these are important, and they work together to make your garden amazing. The DIY Potting Soil Recipe on page 98 contains natural fertilizers (compost and worm castings), and you'll add synthetic fertilizers to your plants as needed.

ACTIVE INGREDIENTS

All fertilizer packages have three big numbers on the front, like 10-10-10 or 4-5-3. These numbers represent the three plant nutrients plants use the most: nitrogen (N), phosphorus (P), and potassium (K). The numbers are always listed in N-P-K order and show the percentage of each nutrient. If you have a 100-pound (45 kg) bag of 10-10-10 fertilizer, it contains 10 pounds (4.5 kg) of nitrogen, 10 pounds (4.5 kg) of phosphorus, and 10 pounds (4.5 kg) of potassium. The remaining 70 pounds (32 kg) are inert materials or other nutrients like iron, copper, manganese, and zinc (which are needed in much smaller amounts).

It's important to know what each of these nutrients does, so you can choose the right fertilizer for your vegetables.

This bell pepper variety should be called "Small But Mighty." There are 10 peppers on this one plant!

Nitrogen

Nitrogen (N) is needed in every cell of a plant. It's important for photosynthesis and promotes vigorous, leafy plant growth. Without enough nitrogen, plants grow slowly, leaves turn pale or yellow and may die. Areas between the leaf veins may turn yellow. Apply too much nitrogen and you end up with large, dark green, leafy plants and no flowers or fruit.

Phosphorus

Phosphorus (P) is used by plants to make flowers, fruits, and seeds. Soil often has enough phosphorus, but plants can't absorb it unless the soil is in the right pH range (acid or alkaline level), and calcium and potassium are present. Phosphorus deficiency is indicated by stunted or slow growth, dark purple coloration, or early fruit drop. Excess phosphorus interferes with the plants' absorption of calcium, so plants will have browning leaves and poor fruit production.

Potassium

Potassium (K) enhances overall growth and helps a plant resist temperature and drought stress. Just as with phosphorus, there is often potassium in the soil, but it is tied up in soil minerals and unavailable to the plants. Without enough potassium, leaves turn brown and curl. Excess potassium prevents the absorption of other nutrients, primarily nitrogen—so the plant will show symptoms of nitrogen deficiency (see above).

Potatoes require a deep container and need to be fertilized infrequently during the growing season.

What do the benefits of fertilizing look like in action?

This is a healthy tomato plant, full of flowers, and with loads of tomatoes. Compare it with this picture from a few years ago, when I used a fertilizer with lots of nitrogen. The plants are huge and bushy, but there are no flowers or tomatoes to be seen.

LIQUID OR DRY

Fertilizers are made in liquid form and also in granular, or dry, form. Both types provide nutrients, so deciding which type to use is simply a matter of preference. Liquid fertilizers are usually mixed with water and poured onto the soil (not onto the leaves—see foliar feeding, below). Dry fertilizers are mixed into the top layer of soil and then the plant is watered to activate the fertilizer.

WHAT SHOULD I USE?

The decision about which fertilizer(s) to use is based on what you're growing, of course. Fruit trees need different nutrients than vegetables, which need different fertilizers than lawns and flowers. That said, for growing vegetables, fruits, and herbs I use Sure Start 4-6-2 fertilizer when planting, and liquid fish and kelp fertilizer throughout the growing season.

How to Apply Fertilizer

Always follow the package instructions when applying fertilizer, and don't overfertilize. Too much fertilizer will hurt your plants much more than underfertilizing! Remember, if you are using a high-quality potting soil to fill your containers, there may already be fertilizer in it. Read the label so you don't overfertilize. If the potting soil does indeed have fertilizer in it, you may not need to add additional fertilizer until 4 to 6 weeks into the growing season.

SIDE DRESSING

This is the best way to fertilize container plants. Side dressing means to apply liquid or dry, granular fertilizer to the soil next to actively growing plants. If you're applying liquid fertilizer, dilute it according to label instructions and pour it onto the soil with a watering can or hose-end spray nozzle. If you're using dry fertilizer, sprinkle a small amount of fertilizer on the soil. Wear gardening gloves or use an old spoon to handle the fertilizer. Use a fork or another small tool to mix the dry fertilizer into the top layer of soil, then water the plant thoroughly.

TOP DRESSING

This is the way lawns are usually fertilized—by sprinkling fertilizer over the surface of the plant. This is not a good idea for container gardens, because if any fertilizer sticks to the wet leaves the plant could get a chemical burn.

FOLIAR FEED

As you can tell by the name, this method describes spraying liquid fertilizer on the foliage, or leaves, of the plant. It's not the best method of feeding your plants because only very small amounts of nutrients can enter a plant through the leaf tissue—the benefit actually happens when the fertilizer drips off the leaves and into the soil. If you choose to foliar feed, be sure to dilute the fertilizer as directed so it won't burn your plant leaves.

Apply granular fertilizer to the soil at the side of the plant, mix it into the soil, and then water the plant thoroughly.

LEFT: A vertical garden can fit nearly anywhere. These fabric grow pouches contain a colorful variety of salad greens that can be fertilized by mixing a dry granular fertilizer into the soil or by using a liquid fertilizer throughout the growing season.

Fertilizer tips

Protect your plants and your planet by using fertilizer properly and safely in your container garden:

- Fertilize in the early morning or early evening when plants aren't stressed from the heat of the day.

- If you spill dry fertilizer, sweep it up and throw it away. Washing fertilizer into storm drains causes it to contaminate streams, lakes, and rivers.

- Too much fertilizer can burn or kill plants. It's better to apply diluted fertilizer more often than to pour a bunch of fertilizer in the soil all at once.

- Don't use lawn fertilizer on vegetables. Lawn fertilizer has too much nitrogen for vegetables, and it may contain weed control chemicals that will kill your plants.

Fertilize early in the day, if possible, before heat stress occurs and when your plants are their strongest.

Soil Amendments

When you're at the garden store, you may see bags marked soil amendment next to bags of potting soil. There is definitely a difference between these two items, and they are not interchangeable. Amendments are organic materials that you add to the soil to improve soil health. As you learned in Chapter 4, soil contains minerals, organic matter, water, and air. The organic matter contains plant and animal residues in various stages of decomposition; organisms like earthworms, fungi, and bacteria; and other substances. The proper ratios of minerals, organic matter, water, and air are what make soil fertile and able to grow plants.

COMMON SOIL AMENDMENTS AND NATURAL FERTILIZERS

There are lots and lots of soil amendments, including natural fertilizers, at the garden center. This chart will help you identify what they do and whether you need to use them in your container garden. Or if someone says, "Hey, I heard you should add such-and-such to your soil" you'll know how to answer them.

Soil Amendments and Fertilizers

NAME	WHAT IT'S MADE OF	WHAT IT DOES
Bat guano	Bat poop	Adds nitrogen and phosphorus. Harvesting methods negatively affect bats and cave ecosystems.
Blood meal	Powder made from animal blood	Adds nitrogen; can be toxic to pets if large amounts are ingested.
Bone meal	Powder made from animal bones	Adds phosphorus; can be toxic to pets if large amounts are ingested.
Coco coir	Ground coconut husk fiber, a natural by-product of coconut processing	Retains moisture, aerates soil.
Compost	Decaying plant material	Adds nutrients, improves soil structure, adds beneficial microbes and bacteria to protect plants from disease.
Fish meal	Powder made from dried and ground fish	Adds nitrogen and phosphorus slowly into the soil.
Kelp or kelp meal	Dried and ground seaweed	Provides multiple trace minerals, improves soil structure, and is very gentle on plants.
Leaves or leaf mold	Shredded and/or decomposed tree leaves	Improves soil structure and texture, retains moisture. It takes from 1–3 years for leaf piles to break down into leaf mold.
Manure	Composted herbivore poop	Improves soil structure, provides nutrients. Do not use fresh manure because it will burn plants and may contain harmful bacteria. Always fully compost manure before using it.
Peat moss	Compressed and partially decomposed sphagnum moss	Aerates soil and retains moisture. Peat moss is mined and takes centuries to replenish naturally.
Perlite	A specific type of volcanic glass that puffs when heated	Improves soil aeration in containers.
Rice hulls	Husks of rice that are removed after harvest	Improves soil drainage and aeration, improves water retention.
Vermiculite	A silicate mineral that expands when heated	Retains water
Worm castings	Earthworm poop	Provides many nutrients and adds beneficial microbes and bacteria to protect plants from disease.

AMENDMENTS TO AVOID

Gardeners love to share their successes and ideas with others. However, some suggestions don't hold up when they're put to the test. Here are some soil amendments to avoid:

Antacid tablets: Theoretically antacid tablets prevent blossom end rot when added to the soil because they contain water-soluble calcium. However, blossom end rot happens because the plant can't absorb the calcium already in the soil because it isn't being watered regularly (see Chapter 8 for the details).

Coffee grounds: These may acidify the soil, but chemicals in coffee can inhibit the growth of some plants. It's best to add coffee grounds to your compost pile instead of directly into the garden.

Eggshells: It's often recommended to dry eggshells, crush, and add them to the garden. The idea is the calcium in the eggshells will enrich the soil and prevent blossom end rot. However, blossom end rot isn't caused by a lack of calcium, but the inability of the plant to absorb calcium due to inconsistent watering (see Chapter 8).

Epsom salt: Magnesium sulfate is great for gardeners—when you soak your feet in an Epsom salt bath after a long day of working in the garden. If your plants need these micronutrients (which is unlikely) they'll get them from the compost or worm castings you're already using.

Sawdust and wood chips: In container plantings, sawdust and wood chips are slow to break down and can rob the uppermost layer of soil of nitrogen, which container-grown plants need for healthy growth.

Adding amendments or fertilizers can improve the health of your soil and the plants growing in it.

Mulch

Mulch is simply a layer of opaque material spread over the soil surface. Mulching your in-ground garden is a vital step in growing healthy vegetables. But did you know it's also useful in a container garden? In fact, it's one of the best all-natural ways to protect your plants and help them thrive. There are lots of benefits to using mulch in your container garden. Here are some of the best reasons to mulch your pots:

- Mulch acts as a barrier to retain moisture in container soil.

- Mulch protects the soil (and roots of your plants) from drastic temperature shifts.

- Mulch prevents soil loss from irrigation runoff.

- Mulch suppresses weeds, which isn't a huge factor in container gardens, but occasionally weed seeds are blown in or are brought in on compost.

- Over time, high-quality natural mulch will break down and add nutrients to the soil. This is especially important for perennial edibles that will be growing in their container for more than one season.

Mulching the soil in your containers has many benefits, the most important of which is reducing the need to water. This container is mulched with straw.

WHICH MULCHES NOT TO USE

Not all mulches are created equal. Some are not food safe, like rubber mulch, and others just aren't suited for a container garden.

Here are the mulches you want to avoid using:

Rubber Mulch

Rubber mulch from recycled tires is sometimes considered eco-friendly because it's recycled and can be used in large-scale applications. However, it also comes with some very big problems:

- Rubber mulch doesn't decompose. This means it doesn't add nutrients to your container like natural mulch. It also means you can't safely work it into the container garden soil like natural mulches.

- Rubber mulch contains many toxins. Recycled tires are not natural whatsoever. Commercial rubber is processed and treated with chemicals you definitely don't want in your food garden, and this mulch may also contain heavy metals that leach into the soil.

Wood Chips

Although wood chips and shredded bark are natural, they're not the best choice for a container garden. Wood chips have the tendency to absorb nitrogen from the upper surface layers of soil. This isn't a problem for trees, shrubs, and perennials planted in the ground, but it can cause problems with container vegetables because of the finite amount of soil the plant can access. Nitrogen is important for plant growth, so don't deplete the soil by using wood chips in your containers.

Another problem with wood chips is that many commercial wood mulches are chemically treated or dyed, and these chemicals can leach into the soil. So even though wood is a natural material, sometimes the wood used for mulch has been treated with substances that are definitely *not* food safe. Leonardo the tortoise says, "Skip those dyed black, red, or blue wood chips, please!"

Black Plastic

Plastic mulch can work for containers, but it isn't very attractive. While it's functional, I don't recommend it for containers. It's not eco-friendly, is a pain to install and remove, and it tends to break down over time and make a mess.

Rubber Mulch

Wood Chips

Black Plastic

THE BEST CONTAINER VEGETABLE GARDEN MULCHES

Now it's time to dig into the topic of which types of mulch will work best in your container vegetable garden. Since container gardens have newly established plants with shallow roots (and they're plants you intend to eat!), you want to be extra careful about choosing the right mulch.

Here are the best natural mulches for your container garden:

Pine Needles or Pine Straw

Pine straw is an excellent organic mulch that's both eco-friendly and budget friendly. It's especially good for plants that love acidic soil, such as celery, carrots, cucumbers, squash, pumpkin, blueberries, and peppers. Pine straw tends to weave together, so it won't blow away too easily. It also decomposes slowly and will last a long time in containers.

Pine Needles

Applying mulch

Once you've decided on the type of mulch you're using, it's easy to add it to your containers. If you're growing from seed, wait until the plant has sprouted and is a few inches tall. If you're growing from seedlings, you can apply mulch right after planting.

Here's how:

- Water the soil, using the low and slow method on page 120.
- Lift up the bottom leaves of the plant and spread the mulch evenly over the soil to a depth of about 2 inches (5 cm).
- Keep the mulch away from the stem of the plant. This helps prevent rot and promotes air circulation.
- If using a lightweight mulch like straw or shredded leaves, spray the mulch with water to help it stay in place.

After a few months, the mulch will break down into the soil. Add another layer right on top of the old mulch, being sure to keep it away from the stem.

Curious critters (mice, squirrels, toddlers) may dig up the mulch to bury nuts or to eat plant roots and bulbs. Discourage them from digging with the tips beginning on page 162.

Before fertilizing, move the mulch aside so the nutrients go directly into the soil. Then replace the mulch and add more if needed.

Straw

Regular straw (not hay, which contains seeds) is also a great all-natural mulch for containers. It's inexpensive and easy to apply. It also does a great job of protecting the soil and retaining moisture. The biggest drawbacks of straw are the possibility of seed contamination (which can lead to weed growth), and its tendency to blow away with any breeze. If you spray it with water soon after putting it in place, it will stay put better.

Shredded Leaves

Dry, shredded leaves make a nutrient-rich, organic mulch that both feeds and protects the soil. It's also a great way to recycle fall leaves. Leaf mulch doesn't last as long as other mulches because it decomposes quickly, but that's also why it's perfect for containers where it will be replaced yearly. Just make sure the leaves are dry and shredded (you can shred them with a lawn mower). Apply a layer of shredded leaves to the container and spray them with water so they don't blow away easily.

Dry Grass Clippings

Grass clippings are also another good material to recycle from your yard. Grass clippings are free if you bag them from your own yard, and they decompose easily to add nutrients and organic matter to the soil.

Two things to remember when using grass clippings as natural mulch in your containers:

- Don't use clippings from grass that has been chemically treated with fertilizers or insecticides. You don't want those chemicals in your food!

- Dry grass clippings work best. Freshly cut grass can hold too much moisture and create a matted, moldy mess in the pot (not to mention the smell). I let the clippings dry on the lawn and then rake them up when I need them.

Cardboard

This probably sounds like a strange recommendation, but cardboard is actually a great biodegradable mulch for pots. Use plain brown cardboard for mulching projects—nothing waxy or glossy. Run the cardboard through your paper shredder to get nice, even pieces, or if you have a large container, simply cut wedges or half-circles of solid cardboard to surround the plant. Wet the cardboard thoroughly so it stays in place.

LEFT: Straw

Shredded Leaves

Dry Grass Clippings

Cardboard

8

Troubleshooting

Don't Panic! This is the most important thing to remember when something's not right in your container garden. Every gardener—no matter how famous or successful—has had garden problems of one kind or another. Maybe their puppy sat in the planter with their new tree, or maybe the slugs ate more strawberries than they did.

Problems happen from time to time, but they can almost always be fixed or prevented to ensure future successful harvests. Container gardens have a big advantage over in-ground gardens because the plants can be treated and moved individually. For example, you can easily quarantine a container tomato with spider mites by moving the container to a different part of your space. In an in-ground garden, that would be impractical (at best) and deadly to the tomato plant (at worst).

This section shares some common garden problems and easy, natural ways to solve them. It's divided into three sections: plants, insects, and animals.

- **The plant problems section** tackles problems with the plants' stems and leaves, and problems with the vegetables or fruits themselves.

- **The insect pest problems section** shows good and bad garden bugs, and how to deal with them when they appear.

- **The deterring animals section** recommends ways to deter all kinds of four-legged creatures from invading your garden.

Seedlings Have Disappeared

This can happen literally overnight, usually to just-sprouted seedlings. They'll be growing happily one day and the next day they're gone.

There are a couple of causes for this—if the stems are cut off at soil level, it's probably cutworms. If the plant has been dug up, a rodent is likely the culprit.

If you find cutworm damage in your container garden, be sure you're using commercial or homemade potting soil. Reusing soil from your in-ground garden may bring buried cutworms into your containers.

Symptoms

The parts of the plant above the surface of the soil are gone. There may still be roots or a bit of stem underground.

Solutions

- Unfortunately, once a seedling is cut off, it can't be revived. Replace the soil in your container if possible, and plant new seeds or seedlings. Place a barrier (like a toilet paper tube) around the seedling to protect it.

- Don't use garden soil in your containers because there may be cutworms in the soil. Use commercial or homemade container gardening soil instead.

- Apply *Bacillus thuringiensis* (also called Bt), which is a natural bacterium that targets cutworms, caterpillars, and other bugs. Reapply after rain.

Protect seedlings from being eaten by cutworms by placing half of a toilet paper tube around each seedling.

White Powder on Leaves

White or gray powdery spots can sometimes appear on plants' leaves, making them look like they've been dusted with flour. This is called powdery mildew, which is a fungal infection exacerbated by humidity, wet leaves, low light, and crowded plants.

Symptoms

Pale yellow leaf spots that become white or gray and powdery; the spots can quickly engulf the leaves and stems. While powdery mildew itself isn't usually fatal to plants, it can impede photosynthesis if left unchecked.

Solutions

- Powdery mildew is easier to prevent than to control. Always water edible plants at the soil level rather than from above and ensure they have at least 6 hours of sunlight per day.

- Choose disease-resistant varieties when planting.

- Spray leaves weekly with a mixture of one cup (236 ml) cow's milk to two cups (475 ml) water.

- Cut off any affected leaves, stems, and fruit and throw them away. Don't compost them because the fungus spores can lay dormant and reappear. Wipe your pruning shears with rubbing alcohol after pruning.

Leaves that appear to be dusted with flour are infected with powdery mildew.

Leaves Turning Brown

Leaves can turn brown for many reasons, most of which are fixable. Some of the most common culprits are problems with watering, overfertilizing, or freezing temperatures.

Symptoms

The tips of leaves turn brown, eventually leading to the entire leaf turning brown.

Solutions

- The plant may not have enough water. Check the soil and water if needed. If the soil has dried out and the water runs off the surface, either soak the entire container in water or poke holes in the soil with a long stick or screwdriver.

- The leaves could be burned from overapplication of fertilizer or pesticides (either applying too often or at too high of a concentration). If this is the case, flush the soil with water and add compost.

- If freezing temperatures have damaged the plant, protect it from future freezes by moving it to a warmer microclimate.

This vegetable leaf is turning brown due to misuse of a homemade insecticide mixture.

Yellowing Leaves

This can be a tricky one! Yellowing leaves are due to plant stress, but you must do some detective work to figure out the root of the problem (pun intended).

Symptoms

Individual leaves turn yellow, or the entire plant begins to turn yellow from the soil up.

Solutions

- Check the soil moisture to ensure plants aren't too dry or too wet. If using a saucer or cachepot, be sure to empty it after watering.

- If the yellowing starts at the bottom of the plant and moves upward, the plant needs more nitrogen. Apply fertilizer or compost.

- Check the plant for pests like aphids, spider mites, squash borers, or others.

These snow pea leaves are turning yellow due to lack of water and warmer temperatures, both of which cause stress to this cold-weather plant.

Large, Ragged Holes in Leaves

There are a few different suspects in this mystery, but in my garden, many times earwigs, snails, or slugs are the culprit. A slime trail indicates that the snails or slugs are the guilty party. All these critters can and will eat the vegetables as well as the leaves, so they've gotta go.

Symptoms

Large holes with irregular edges on leaves, or damage to young, tender seedlings.

Solutions

- Sprinkle a ring of diatomaceous earth on the soil around the base of the affected plant. Reapply after watering or rain.

- Get rid of snails and slugs by sprinkling iron phosphate pellets around the plant. Iron phosphate is poisonous to snails and slugs but doesn't harm people or pets (unless eaten in large quantities).

The large holes in the leaves of this pole bean plant are likely due to a leaf-munching pest.

Squiggly Lines on Leaves

Leaves that have white or yellow squiggly lines that look like doodles are not due to bugs being bored during a meeting, but rather because leaf miner larvae are eating their way through the leaves. While the damage is cosmetic, a bad leaf miner infestation can weaken the plant and reduce yield. If the plant is grown for its leaves (spinach, chard, etc.) then leaf miner damage can ruin the entire crop.

Leaf miner larvae overwinter in the soil, so if you're using new potting soil you probably won't encounter these pests.

Symptoms

White or yellow squiggly lines on leaves, sometimes extending into larger blotches.

Solutions

- Because the larvae are eating the tissue inside the leaves, pesticides and sprays often don't work.

- Pick and discard infected leaves. Don't compost them because the larvae could survive and begin the cycle again.

Squiggly lines on leaves, sometimes becoming large blotches of damage, are due to leaf miner larvae.

Wilted Leaves

It's normal for vegetable leaves to wilt slightly in the heat of the afternoon. If the plant doesn't perk up by the morning, though, there could be another problem. Wilted leaves on squash plants (pumpkin, zucchini, winter squash) could indicate squash vine borers. These garden pests need to be removed before they destroy your plants (see the Insect section of this chapter). If this is occurring on your cucumber plants, it could be bacterial wilt, which is spread by the cucumber beetle.

Symptoms

Leaves droop and sag during the heat of the day, especially in late afternoon. If not remedied, can cause permanent damage and plant death.

Solutions

- Check the soil; if dry, water the plant thoroughly. Be sure to drain any standing water under the container.

- If a squash plant's leaves are wilted, check the stem carefully for squash borers.

- For cucumber plants, select varieties that are resistant to bacterial wilt and plant burpless varieties that are less attractive to the cucumber beetles that transmit the disease.

This squash plant's leaves are wilted from the hot afternoon sun. If the plant is healthy, it will recover by morning.

Holes in the Soil/Bite Marks in Fruit

If you find divots or shallow holes in your container soil or bite marks on your vegetables, you've probably had rodent visitors. These furry critters (squirrels, rats, voles, and mice) can wreak havoc on your garden. Squirrels will dig in containers to bury nuts, and mice, rats, and voles will eat your vegetables.

Symptoms

There are divots or shallow holes in container soil, sometimes with uprooted plants nearby. Vegetables and fruits have bites missing or are completely gone overnight.

Solutions

- Install a cylinder of chicken wire or plastic mesh fencing around the planter.

- If possible, fence in the entire garden area.

- Put a mesh barrier on the soil and let the plants grow through it.

- Protect fruits, like melons and pumpkins, by wrapping them in mesh bags like the ones onions are stored in.

Important! Don't use rodenticides or poisons. These are toxic to pets as well as prey animals that eat rodents.

Holes dug in containers or bites taken from fruit indicate rodent invaders.

Discolored, Leathery Spot on the Base of Fruit

Finally! Your beautiful red tomato is ripe and ready to pick. Then you turn it over and find a sunken leathery black or brown patch on the base of the fruit. This is called blossom end rot, and it can happen to tomatoes, melons, eggplants, peppers, or squash.

Blossom end rot's root cause is a lack of calcium, which is required in relatively large amounts when the fruit is growing. The calcium and other minerals travel through the plant with the help of water. If demand for calcium exceeds supply, or there isn't enough water to deliver the calcium, the plant's tissues break down—especially on the bottom, or blossom end of the fruit.

Symptoms

A brown or black leathery spot on the base of the fruit. While you can cut off the damaged part and eat the rest, I usually compost the offender and wait for the next harvest.

Solutions

- Blossom end rot is almost always caused by fluctuating soil moisture, not a lack of calcium in the soil. This is especially true if you're using container potting soil, which contains plenty of minerals.

- Water regularly and deeply and add mulch to the container to help keep moisture in the soil.

- Blossom end rot can also be caused by overusing synthetic fertilizer that contains ammonia. Instead use natural liquid fertilizers like those containing fish emulsion, kelp, or seaweed.

Important! Don't add Epsom salt, eggshells, antacid tablets, or the like to your container garden. They won't fix blossom end rot and could damage your soil.

Blossom end rot is usually caused by fluctuating soil moisture and can't be cured with Epsom salt, eggshells, or antacid tablets.

Black Crumbs on Tomato Leaves

In the beginning, you'll see what looks like dust or dirt on the tomato leaves. Then leaves start disappearing and sometimes there are holes in the tomatoes. Often the only sign of these voracious tomato and/or tobacco hornworms is the black crumbs of poop they leave behind; they are masters at camouflage.

Symptoms

Leaves with large holes, stems with leaves missing, wilted leaves at the top of the plant. Black or dark green droppings on tomato leaves.

Solutions

- The best way to get rid of tomato and tobacco hornworms is to pick them off by hand. You can squish them or feed them to your chickens or turtle—my turtle loves them.

- If you have several tomatoes in pots near each other, make sure the foliage isn't touching so the hornworms can't easily travel between plants.

- Apply the organic pesticide Bt (*Bacillus thuringiensis*). The hornworms must eat it to be affected. Reapply Bt after rain.

Tomato and tobacco hornworms can be hard to spot on the plant, but you can easily see the damage they cause. These garden pests can be controlled without pesticides.

White or Yellow Patches on Tomatoes and Peppers

While this is sometimes confused with blossom end rot, sunscald usually occurs on the sides or tops of the fruit. Like a sunburn, it happens when fruits that are normally shaded are exposed to direct sun. This is sometimes because insects or disease have damaged the leaves that should be shading the fruit. Sunscald can happen to tomatoes, peppers, melons, and summer squash.

Symptoms

Fruit has sunken, paper-like patches that are white, yellow, or gray. Sometimes cracks will develop, which allows bacteria or fungi to enter. It's safe to eat the undamaged parts.

Solutions

- Fertilize regularly to encourage leaf growth.

- Watch for pests and diseases and start a treatment program right away.

- Use a patio umbrella or other shade cover to protect plants during the hottest part of summer.

A sunken, paper-like patch on a vegetable is a sign of sunscald.

Cucumber or Squash Deformed or Pointy on End

This happens to lots of gardeners, and it's due to poor pollination. The flowers need to be pollinated multiple times to set fruit, and sometimes this doesn't happen. Occasionally extreme heat in the garden will affect the pollen or pollination process. Don't give up on your plants if this happens! Unless it's the end of the growing season, these plants still have a chance to produce healthy fruit.

Symptoms

Fruit is fully developed but tapers down to a point at the blossom end, looking like a long balloon that isn't completely inflated. The rest of the fruit is okay to eat.

Solutions

- Plant flowers and herbs nearby to encourage pollinators to visit.

- Don't use pesticides because they kill pollinators too.

- If you've covered the plant to discourage rodents or pest insects, remove the cover during the day to allow pollinators to visit.

Cucumber flowers must be pollinated several times to set fruit. This one was only partially pollinated, which prevents it from developing completely.

Tomatoes Split or Crack

Tomatoes split when the fruit inside expands faster than the skin. This happens when the tomato plant gets a lot of water all at once, especially after a prolonged dry period. Then the fruit inside swells with water before the skin has time to grow.

A heavy rain is the usual culprit, but you could potentially cause tomatoes to crack if you overwater them suddenly during a dry period.

Symptoms

Tomatoes split or crack down the sides. Some heirloom varieties have superficial cracks near the stem, and these aren't caused by overwatering. As long as there's no mold or insect damage, the rest of the fruit is okay to eat.

Solutions

- Regular watering is one of the best ways to prevent tomatoes from cracking open. Give your tomatoes 1–2 inches (3–5 cm) of water once per week to keep them hydrated.

- Another solution is to add 2–3 inches (5–8 cm) of mulch around your tomato plants. Mulch holds moisture in the soil, which prevents the cycle of tomatoes being too dry then too wet.

- Fertilize tomatoes every two weeks. Feeding your tomatoes regularly keeps them healthy and their growth consistent.

- Some varieties of tomatoes are more prone to cracking than others. Select crack-resistant types for your container garden.

Tomatoes can split after overwatering. This happens when the fruit's flesh expands faster than the skin.

Aphids

Aphids are very small bugs that feed on plant juices. They can be white, brown, gray, or light green.

Damage

You'll know you have aphids when you see them on your plants, see misshapen or curled leaves, or if the leaves are covered with a sticky substance. This is politely called honeydew, but it's actually aphid poop. The honeydew can attract ants, who gather it for food.

Solutions

- In the morning, spray the underside of the affected leaves with a blast of water from the hose. The spray of water will dislodge the aphids from the plant, and they'll fall to their untimely demise.

- Apply neem oil. This natural pesticide keeps the aphids from feeding, prevents nymphs from maturing, and suffocates the aphids on the plant.

- Insecticidal soap (not dish soap or laundry soap) can be used with care right up until harvest. It suffocates the aphids and helps wash off the honeydew that the aphids excrete.

While a few aphids aren't cause for concern, it's best to get rid of them before they overwhelm the garden.

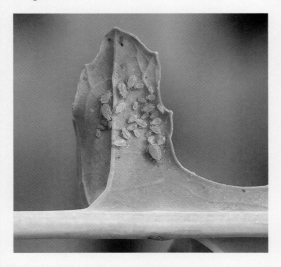

Earwigs

Earwigs are small, flat-bodied insects with unmistakable pinchers on their tail end. Also called pincher bugs, they're dark brown in color and often found in cool, dark places—including beneath garden debris, pots, mulch, and leaves.

Damage

Earwigs like to feast on decaying plant matter of all kinds but will also target seedlings and leaves (they love lettuce). This is what makes them a particular nuisance in the garden.

Solutions

- If possible, put your containers on the deck or patio instead of on grass or soil. Earwigs can't travel far in dry conditions.

- Sprinkle a ring of diatomaceous earth on the soil around the base of the affected plant. This will repel the earwigs, but it needs to be reapplied after watering or rain.

- Set a shallow can filled with soy sauce and vegetable oil into the soil at the base of the plant. The earwigs will fall in and drown.

Earwigs make circular holes in plant leaves, just like snails and slugs. If you see these holes without a slime trail, earwigs are the culprit.

Snails and Slugs

Easily recognizable and the bane of every gardener, snails and slugs destroy seedlings and munch holes in plants. They are known as gastropods, which comes from the ancient Greek meaning "stomach foot." This is an apt description since they ooze along on a muscular foot eating everything in their path.

Damage

Snails and slugs leave large, ragged holes in the leaves, vegetables, and fruits they eat. Their damage looks similar to that of earwigs or caterpillars. The giveaway for snails and slugs (besides seeing them, of course), is the slime trail they leave behind. Look for that first.

Solutions

- Sink an old tuna can into the soil and fill it with beer. The snails and slugs will crawl in and drown—but this method unfortunately requires that you eat several cans of tuna and "waste" a can of beer.

- Sprinkle iron phosphate slug bait pellets around the plant. Iron phosphate is a stomach poison for snails and slugs but doesn't harm people or pets (unless eaten in large quantities).

- Handpick and crush them or throw them away.

Important! Don't use traditional snail baits that contain metaldehyde as the active ingredient. This chemical is a neurotoxin and is toxic to dogs, cats, and birds.

Snails and slugs leave large, ragged holes in leaves, and a telltale slime trail in their wake.

Tomato and Tobacco Hornworms

Damage

These tomato killers are masters at camouflage and can cause serious damage to your plants. They are green caterpillars with white stripes and a large "horn" or spike on the end. They eat tomato leaves, tomatoes, and sometimes peppers and eggplant. They can eat so many leaves that the fruit is susceptible to sunscald.

Solutions

- The best way to get rid of hornworms is to pick them off by hand. Squish them, or—if you haven't used any pesticides—feed them to your chickens or turtle.

- If you have several tomatoes in pots near each other, separate them so the hornworms can't travel between plants.

- Apply the organic pesticide Bt (*Bacillus thuringiensis*), but the hornworms must eat it to be affected. Reapply Bt after rain.

Camouflaged hornworms can be hard to find on your plants. Search the upper ends of branches and stems for a green caterpillar with white stripes and a large "horn" or spike on the end.

Squash Borer

These annoying pests are the larvae of the squash vine borer. The pupae overwinter in the soil, so you're unlikely to encounter them if you're using new potting soil. Because they eat the squash vine from the inside, they're hard to find and hard to control.

Damage

Leaves of squash plants (pumpkin, zucchini, and winter squash) are wilted in the morning. There's a hole chewed in the stem at the soil level and sawdust-like poop near the stem. If you cut the stem open, you'll find the fat larvae in there eating away.

Solutions

- Prevention is easier than eradication. Put a thin strip of aluminum foil around the bottom of the stem—you'll need to replace it a couple of times as the plant grows.

- Sprinkle diatomaceous earth around the stalks when the vines are small or in early to mid-summer.

- If you find the telltale hole in the vine, you can carefully split the vine open with a sharp knife and extract or squish the offending larvae.

This squash borer larvae can destroy a squash plant in days. Prevention is the best solution.

Ladybugs

Ladybugs are cute and adorable to us, but if you're an aphid—look out! One ladybug can eat its weight in aphids every single day (that's about 50 aphids per ladybug). They also eat whiteflies and mites, making them a valuable predator in your garden.

Ladybug larvae look like tiny prehistoric monsters. During their 2–3 week larvae stage, one of these little critters will eat about 400 aphids.

In addition to insects, ladybugs eat nectar. Plant extra cilantro, dill, fennel, or chives and let them go to flower. This will encourage the ladybugs to stay in your garden.

Ladybugs can eat their weight in aphids each day. This one is headed up a parsley stem to eat the aphids that are just below the flower buds.

These are ladybug larvae. They're aphid-eating machines and are a welcome visitor to your garden.

Praying Mantis

When you think "good bug," these big, leggy insects often come to mind. They'll eat moths, crickets, grasshoppers, and flies, as well as any good bugs they come across—including each other.

Praying mantises are territorial, so you'll usually find one lone mantis sitting camouflaged on a plant. It will stay on that plant as long as food is available. While waiting for its prey to happen by, the mantis waits with its front legs folded like it's praying. Once an insect is in reach, it strikes out in a flash and grabs its victim.

Praying mantises cover their eggs in a foamy substance that forms an ootheca or egg case. The ootheca looks like a light brown, papery bundle. If you see one on a tree branch or fence, leave it be. The mantis babies will hatch when the weather is warm.

Praying mantises can turn their heads 180 degrees to search for prey in your garden.

A praying mantis egg case, called an ootheca, can be attached to tree branches, fences, or other structures in the garden. This one is for the Chinese mantid, an introduced species here in North America.

Parasitic Wasps

Are you surprised to hear that wasps are a beneficial insect? These are! Parasitic wasps are several species of tiny, nonstinging wasps that lay their eggs inside of or on specific host insects. When the eggs hatch, the larvae eat the host. You may see a tomato hornworm with white sacs on its back that look like grains of rice—those are the pupae of a species of braconid wasp.

Parasitic wasps prey on a variety of pests, including aphids, cutworms, squash borers, tomato hornworms, cabbage loopers, and codling moths, depending on the wasp species. Attract them to your garden by allowing herbs like dill, fennel, and cilantro to go to flower.

These tiny wasps are no danger to humans—you're more likely to see evidence of them on caterpillars or aphids than you are to see the wasps themselves.

Bees

After hosting a beehive in our backyard for a few years, I have many wonderful things to say about honeybees. Our garden performed incredibly thanks to their help, and we got to enjoy their delicious honey. There are many different kinds of bees, and they're all valuable pollinators. My favorites are the giant black carpenter bees, whose wings are so loud it sounds like an airplane going by.

Many of the vegetables and fruits in your garden need to be pollinated several times in order to produce—so the more bees you have, the better. Attract them to your garden by planting flowers like sweet alyssum and bee balm, or let your dill, oregano, and thyme plants go to flower.

Happy honeybees headed inside our backyard hive. These pollinators are a welcome visitor to any garden.

Spiders

Spiders are voracious eaters who will help eliminate many different pests in your container garden. They eat many insects including mosquitoes, aphids, caterpillars, cucumber beetles, flies, grasshoppers, leafhoppers, and thrips. They might occasionally catch a beneficial insect or two, but if they're catching mosquitoes, I figure the tradeoff is worth it.

Encourage spiders to spin webs in your garden by including tall structures like sunflowers and tomato cages. Hunting spiders (species that do not spin webs) can often be found crawling around on soil and plants, looking for prey.

Garden spiders spin webs and capture many garden pests—including mosquitoes.

Green Lacewing

Green lacewings have a thin, green body and pretty, transparent wings. The adults feed on nectar, pollen, and honeydew, so adding flowers to your container garden will help attract them. They are active at night and tolerate wide temperature ranges and can be found in the garden throughout most of the growing season.

Green lacewing larvae are serious pest predator and use pincer-like mandibles to grab and eat their prey. They feed on many small insects, including aphids, thrips, whitefly, leafhoppers, mites, and mealybugs. One green lacewing larva can eat more than 200 insects per week!

This delicate beauty is a green lacewing, who— along with its larvae—eat many garden pests.

Whether you're in the city or the country, there are critters out there that could attack your garden. Squirrels and deer are looking for a free lunch and cats might think your container is their own personal litterbox. Here are some ways to keep these pests out of your garden.

Cats

For the most part, cats aren't interested in the plants you're growing; they just like to use the fresh soil as a litterbox. You need to keep them away from your container garden until the plants are big enough to cover the soil. Here's how:

Solutions

- Lay sticks across the top of the containers.
- Place plastic garden fencing on the surface of the soil and remove it before the plants get too big.
- Rig a temporary fence or barrier around the container that's too high for the cat to jump over.
- Cover the soil with mulch, which makes it unappealing for cats to dig in.

Don't use these commonly recommended methods:

- Cayenne pepper: many commercial animal repellents contain this ingredient. It can burn a cat's paws, mouth, and eyes, and cause diarrhea and vomiting.
- Mothballs: mothballs are a pesticide and are toxic to pets, people, and wildlife.
- Plastic forks: you've probably seen a picture with an army of forks sticking up from the soil. This is bad for several reasons: plastic silverware is bad for the environment; it looks tacky as all heck; and some plastics, when heated, can leach toxins into the soil.
- Coffee grounds: even a small amount of coffee grounds, if ingested, can kill a cat or dog. Please don't use coffee grounds in your garden. Put them in your compost pile instead.

Cats and gardens aren't a good combination. These fuzzy felines can squish your plants or may use the soil as a litterbox.

Rodents and Rabbits

Squirrels, chipmunks, mice, rats, and rabbits can wreak havoc in your garden. These little chaos beasts will take bites out of vegetables and fruits, dig holes in containers, and make a giant mess while doing so. Physical barriers are the best way to deter them:

Solutions

- Cover plants with medium-size mesh netting having holes that are big enough for pollinators but too small for critters to get through.
- If your bird feeder attracts squirrels, move it as far away from the container garden as possible.
- Keep critters away from melons, pumpkins, and other desirables by wrapping the ripening fruits in mesh bags (like the ones onions are sold in).
- Cover the soil with mulch, which they don't like to walk on or dig in.
- Some natural deer repellant sprays will keep rodents away as well.

Don't use these methods:

- Poison bait or rodenticides: these are harmful to kids, pets, and prey animals.
- Live traps: in many cases it's illegal to relocate the animal, and another one will simply take its place.
- Dogs/cats: these are great at keeping rodents away, but adopting a pet is a serious commitment and shouldn't be done just for the purpose of protecting your garden.

Rabbits and other critters will help themselves to your container plants but can be dissuaded with simple physical barriers.

Deer

We don't have many problems with deer in the city, but rural and suburban gardeners have been fighting them off for ages. Deer are hungry creatures and can eat a garden to the ground in short order. Here are some humane ways to keep them away from your container garden:

Solutions

• Surround your garden with an 8 foot (2.4 m) or taller fence.

• Protect individual plants or containers with bird netting.

• Use a natural deer repellant spray that's made from dried animal blood or rotten eggs and reapply it regularly. However, don't use these repellants on plant parts you plan to eat as the foul taste will linger on your harvest. Hanging repellants may be a better idea for food gardens.

Skip these deer repellent methods:

• Bars of soap or clumps of human hair: these are reputed to keep deer away because of their smell, but they don't actually work. They look slightly ridiculous as well.

• Predator or human urine: this is frequently recommended online. Aside from the privacy issues around using your garden as a bathroom, the use of predator urine has been studied and found ineffective.

• Fishing line tripwires surrounding the garden: while these might repel deer, I'm 100% confident that I'll forget about them, trip, and fall flat on my face. Use with caution.

Deer are opportunistic munchers and will eat just about anything they can find—like these roses.

Conclusion

Congratulations! You've unlocked all the information you need to create your very first container vegetable garden. I encourage you to jump in and get started, even if it's just a single plant on your windowsill. Yes, it takes more time to get a garden started than it takes to go to the store and buy vegetables. But your garden will give you satisfaction that you cannot buy. Sowing seeds, tending plants with care, and sharing your harvest with family and friends is an amazing experience.

I hope you've enjoyed following my family's garden journey through these pages. Over the years, we've gone from a couple of herbs on the windowsill to an abundant food forest in our tiny city yard. The garden has taught us different lessons every season, and we continue to learn and grow year after year.

You're now a gardener—part of a worldwide group of folks who love to share seeds, plants, and advice, and we welcome you with open arms. As you head outside to get your garden started, know this:

- You're a gardener whether you grow one plant on your windowsill or you harvest enough zucchini to feed a small country.

- You're a gardener if all your seeds sprout, but you're still a gardener if they don't.

- You're a gardener even if your harvest doesn't match the fancy pictures online. Enjoy every delicious bite.

You Got This!

Glossary

This glossary is not an exhaustive list of gardening terms and definitions, but it will clarify any terms that aren't defined in the book text.

Annual: a plant that grows, blooms, fruits, and dies within one growing season. Most vegetables and many flowers are annuals, like cucumber and beans.

***Bacillus thuringiensis* (Bt):** a microbe found in soil that makes proteins that are toxic to certain insect larvae.

Biennial: a plant that grows leaves the first year and flowers/sets seed the second year. Kale and parsley are biennial.

Bolt: some plants, especially cool-season ones eaten for leaves or flower buds (like lettuce or broccoli), bolt when it gets too warm causing them to produce flowers and seed.

Cachepot: a decorative container that conceals a plain container; also called double potting.

Cloche: a bell-shaped cover made of glass or clear plastic that goes over young plants to protect them from wind or frost.

Companion plants: compatible plants that help each other grow better by repelling insects or diseases.

Diatomaceous earth: an all-natural, silica-based powder made from the fossilized remains of tiny creatures called diatoms.

Direct sow: to plant a seed directly into the soil in its permanent growing space.

Dwarf fruits/vegetables: these are smaller-sized plants that produce conventional-sized fruit.

Established: after transplanting, an established plant is one that has started producing new foliage growth—which indicates root growth and a healthy plant.

Frost danger: when temperatures drop below 32 degrees F (0°C) at night, causing ice to form inside plant tissues and damage plant cells.

Fruit: botanically speaking, a fruit is the mature ovary of a flowering plant. Tomatoes, cucumbers, pumpkins, and peppers are technically fruits.

Full sun: a location that receives at least 6 hours of direct sunlight without any shade during that time.

Garden soil: topsoil that has been enriched with compost or other ingredients to make it better for planting. It's dense and doesn't drain water well, which can damage container plants.

Grafted tree: a grafted tree has the roots and trunk of a different, related tree and branches of the desired tree that is grafted to the trunk. Most dwarf fruit trees are grafted to make them smaller and to give them a stronger root system.

Last spring frost: this (average) date varies by location and indicates that there probably won't be any frost in the area until the next fall or winter. Frost is created when the temperature is 32 degrees F (0°C) or below.

Mulch: a specific organic material that has not decomposed. It protects soil, retains water, and prevents weed growth. Mulch is placed on top of the soil around the base of plants.

Partial shade: a location that receives from 3–6 hours of direct sunlight and can have shade in the late afternoon.

Perennial: a plant that grows and produces for a number of years, sometimes dying back to the ground in the winter. Asparagus and artichokes are perennials.

Planting mix: soil that often contains slow-release fertilizers and is designed for growing shrubs or trees. Not recommended for container gardening.

Potting soil: a mixture usually containing peat moss or coco coir, sphagnum moss, bark, perlite, vermiculite, or compost. Drains well and is recommended for container gardening.

Resistant: a plant that's able to resist a certain amount of disease or insect damage.

Rootbound: a plant is rootbound when the roots wind around and around inside the container. Some plants enjoy being rootbound, but most rootbound plants need a larger pot.

Seedling: a young plant grown from seed. Also called a start or a transplant.

Shade: a location that receives fewer than 3 hours of direct sunlight.

Succession plant: planting another crop of the same plant at specific time intervals. This is used for plants that produce all at once, like bush beans, so you always have a new crop coming on.

Topsoil: the uppermost layer of soil on the Earth.

Vegetable: the edible portion of a plant, which could be the leaves, stem, root, etc.

Vermiculite: A silicate mineral that expands when heated and is added to soil to retain water.

Water well until established: after checking the soil for dryness, water as often as needed until the plant produces new growth.

Worm castings: organic fertilizer made from earthworm poop.

About The Author

Pam Farley has been gardening and writing (usually not at the same time) since she was in grade school. These interests collided in 2009, when she started the website BrownThumbMama.com to document her home and garden tips. Now millions of readers from around the world visit her site to learn about vegetable gardening, easy recipes, and making a nontoxic home. When she's not gardening and writing, she's likely camping, reading, or otherwise avoiding housework.

Join Pam online!

Website: BrownThumbMama.com
Facebook: facebook.com/BrownThumbMama
Instagram: instagram.com/BrownThumbMama
YouTube: youtube.com/c/BrownThumbMama

Acknowledgments

Writing this book was a whirlwind experience, which (similar to childbirth) seemed a lot easier once it was over. I'm thankful to the team at Cool Springs Press for guiding me smoothly through this process. Special thanks to Jessica Walliser, my acquisitions editor, who entrusted me with this topic and this series—both are a perfect fit.

Additional thanks to my "supertwin" and hand model, Karyn Williams; the Game Night Gang for their years of support; and my dear friends and mentors, John Angell and Marianne Bird.

And of course, I couldn't have done this without the love and support of my husband Gene and our kids, James and Erin. I love you in every universe.

Photo Credits

Amy Andrychowicz 136

Janet Davis 6, 52 (top), 71, 72 (bottom), 105, 125

Janet Davis, photographer. McCormick Edible Garden Roof, Chicago. 114 (top)

Mark Dwyer 112 (bottom), 114 (bottom), 132, 146 (top left)

Pam Farley 9, 10, 12 (top), 13, 17, 22, 23, 24, 25, 28, 32, 36, 52 (bottom), 72 (top), 73 (bottom), 77 (bottom), 80, 81, 83, 84, 86, 92 (top), 93, 98, 99, 100, 101, 106, 108, 118, 119 (top), 120, 128, 134, 135, 137, 142 (middle), 145 (top and bottom), 148 (left), 149 (right), 150, 152, 153 (right), 154 (right), 156, 157 (left), 158 (left), 159, 160 (right), 168

Sue Goetz 73 (top)

Niki Jabbour 14 (top), 87 (bottom), 95, 144

JLY Gardens 15, 16, 18, 20, 30 (bottom), 50 (right), 66, 70, 75, 85, 94, 96, 102, 110–111, 112 (top), 113, 121, 123, 126, 129, 138, 141, 142 (bottom), 154 (left), 157 (right), 160 (left), 161 (left)

Lisa Roper, photographer. David Mattern, designer. Courtesy of Chanticleer Garden. 4–5

Stephanie Rose 8, 12 (bottom), 14 (bottom), 31, 41, 68, 74, 76 (left), 77 (top), 109 (top), 131 (bottom), 148 (right), 162, 176

Christina Salwitz 76 (right), 78

Shutterstock 19, 26–27, 30 (top), 45–49, 50 (left), 82, 87 (top), 88–89, 90, 107, 109 (bottom), 115, 116, 119 (bottom), 124, 131 (top), 140, 142 (top), 143, 145 (middle), 146 (top right and bottom), 149 (left), 151, 153 (left), 155, 158 (right), 161 (right), 163, 164,

Ashlie Thomas 21

George Weigel 69, 104

Index

drainage and mobility accessories, 83–84

drainage for, 79–84

drainage myths, 83

drainage problems, 82

food-safe materials, 72–78

nonporous materials, 76–77

plants too big for, 77

porous materials, 73–75

rectangular, 87

recycled or upcycled, 78–79

self-watering, about, 79

size and soil volumes chart, 69

square, 87

types to avoid, 78

winterizing, 86

container size, choosing, 52, 68

contamination in food, 12

cucamelon planting guide, 33

cucumber beetle, 151

cucumbers

about, 47

companion and repellant plants, 51

deformed or pointy ends, 154

quick planting guide, 33

wind protection for, 112

cutworms, 148

cylindrical containers, 87

D

deer, 164

diatomaceous earth, 150

dill planting guide, 42

dirt, about, 92

disease resistance, 93

disinfecting containers, 79

drainage

for containers, 79–84

and mobility accessories, 83–84

myths, 83

problems, 82

drain holes

adding to containers, 80–81

clogged, 127

soil loss through, 82

drip lines, 124

drip trays and saucers, 84, 120

dry fertilizers, 135

E

earwigs, 155

eggplant

about, 47

blossom end rot, 152

companion plants, 51

quick planting guide, 33

eggshells, 140

elevation, 113

Environmental Working Group, 30

Epsom salts, 140

F

fabric containers, 73

fences, 112, 164

fertilizers

active ingredients, 134

benefits of, 135

common types of, 139

dry form, 135

how to apply, 137

liquid form, 135

natural vs. synthetic, 133

tips for, 138

fiberglass containers, 77

fig planting guide, 38

fish meal, 139

flowers, for pollinators, 130

foliar feed, 137

food, homegrown, advantages of, 11–12

fruits. *See also specific fruits*

annual, 16

discolored, leathery spots, 152

fruit basket garden, 59

holes and bite marks in, 152

perennial, 16

planting guide, 37–40

troubleshooting, 152–154

full shade, 104

full sun, 104

G

gardening gloves, 26

garden soil, 94

garlic

companion and repellant plants, 51

quick planting guide, 33

glazed ceramic containers, 77

gloves, 26

GMO plants and seeds, 20

Google Earth, 107

grape planting guide, 38

grass clippings, 145

green lacewing, 161

green onion planting guide, 33

greens

best microclimate for, 114

salad garden, 61

smoothie greens garden, 55

H

hand shovel/trowel, 26

heirloom seeds, 20

herbs

annual, 16

attractive to pollinators, 130

biennial, 16

deluxe herb garden, 57

herb planting guide, 42–44

windowsill herb garden, 54

hornworms, 153, 157

hoses, 26

hose with spray nozzle, 122